WILLIE NELSON

Lyrics 1957–1994

WILLIE NELSON

Lyrics 1957–1994

WILLIE NELSON

Don Cusic, Editor

St. Martin's Press

New York

WILLIE NELSON: LYRICS 1957–1994. Copyright © 1995 by Don
Cusic, Editor. All rights reserved. Printed in the United States
of America. No part of this book may be used or reproduced in
any manner whatsoever without written permission except in
the case of brief quotations embodied in critical articles or
reviews. For information, address St. Martin's Press, 175 Fifth
Avenue, New York, N.Y. 10010.

Design by Sara Stemen

LIBRARY OF CONGRESS CATALOGING-IN-PUBLICATION DATA

  Nelson, Willie.
    [Songs. Texts]
    Willie Nelson: lyrics, 1957–1994 / Willie Nelson;   Don
  Cusic, editor.
        p.   cm.
      ISBN 0-312-11917-8
      1. Country music—Texts. I. Cusic, Don. II. Title.
  ML54.6.N45C87   1995 ‹Case›
  782.42′1642′0268—dc20   94-42641
                                                 CIP
                                                 MN

First Edition: March 1995

10   9   8   7   6   5   4   3   2   1

Lovers and madmen have such seething brains,
Such shaping fantasies, that apprehend
More than cool reason ever comprehends.
The lunatic, the lover, and the poet
Are of imagination all compact . . .
The poet's eye, in a fine frenzy rolling,
Doth glance from heaven to earth, from earth to
     heaven;
And as imagination bodies forth
The forms of things unknown, the poet's pen
Turns them to shapes, and gives to aery nothing
A local habitation and a name.

  William Shakespeare, *A Midsummer Night's Dream*

Foreword

I started writing poems when I was about four or five years old and started putting melodies to them as I learned to play some chords on the guitar. I've always wanted to write a lot of songs; in my early days as a songwriter, when I was being pressured to write for material, that was good for me because it really let me prove to myself that I could do it. I know I can; I'll always be able to write songs. But those early days, when I did it in competition with all my peers, were some of the best years I experienced—because it kept me on my toes.

The songs come out pretty much as they are. I've found that if a song is real good I'll remember it; I'll save it and keep it in my mind until I get to a pencil and paper and then I'll write it down. In the early days I had to write most of my songs down right away, because I had to turn them in to publishing companies so they could do lead sheets for other singers. (Before that, I usually put them on a tape recorder.) I work better if I can see the whole picture—and that used to be easier to do. Used to be, you could go into a studio and record a song and get it out in a week or two, but that doesn't happen much anymore.

I don't feel guilty anymore if I don't write something every day. I can't really make myself write; I could go into a room and write something on command, but it wouldn't be worth a damn. I don't want to be forced to settle for a mediocre line rather than going for a line that means something.

I've been a pretty steady writer, I guess. These days, when I write a song I always look back to make sure that it isn't too close to something else I've written. But if I get a good idea for a song, I don't ever question it.

Willie Nelson, 1994

Willie Nelson: His Lyrics

Willie Nelson was inducted into the Country Music Hall of Fame on September 30, 1993. . . . twenty years after his induction into the Nashville Songwriters Hall of Fame. Clearly, he is a man who has had a major impact on country music, and just as clearly that impact began with Willie Nelson the songwriter. It was his writing ambition that brought Willie to Nashville as the 1950s came to a close, and his talent that brought him his first national recognition. Long before his recording and touring efforts paid for themselves, his songs paid the bills.

Country music is a world dominated by words, and the strength of Willie Nelson's songs is in his lyrics. Carried on the waves of Nelson's own sinuous jazz phrasing, they transcend the conventions of songwriting and become personal poetry. Sometimes working within the conventions of meter and rhyme, sometimes challenging them, Nelson is a conscious poet whose form is the country song, who explores his own heart even as he seeks a universal expression any listener can identify with. He has mastered the high-wire act of joining the idiosyncratic and the commercial, and in the process has emerged as something greater than a country artist or a country lyricist. He is a troubador, a poet in the old-world sense of the calling.

His Life

William Hugh Nelson was born on April 30, 1933 in Abbott, Texas, just south of Dallas and Fort Worth. A sleepy Texas town, Abbott looks in parts like a rustic movie set, all dust and big summer Texas sky and wide plains surrounding the town.

If the child is the father to the man, then the key to understanding the grown man is knowing the little boy. Willie Nelson was a boy who lived with a broken heart and a deep, abiding loneliness. His first heartbreak came when his parents divorced, before he was a year old. His grandparents went on to raise Willie and his sister, Bobbi—until just before Willie's seventh birthday, when his grandfather died. His grandmother loved him deeply, but the loss left a deep gap where a strong male figure should have been. He found what consolation he could in the visits of his mother, but they were as painful as they were comforting—Willie would form a close emotional attachment to her every time she came back, only to find her flying off to her home on the West Coast as soon as he'd come to know her again. Countless times Willie stood crying as she drove away.

Yes, most country songs are sad—but Willie Nelson's songs have always been dangerously, seriously sad. Even though they usually seem to be about lovers—and Willie's immediate inspiration was often a current love—most are also invested with that dark childhood heartbreak.

Nelson remembers that he began writing songs when he was seven years old, just after his grandfather died; they were songs about "cheating," he recalls, "infidelity and betrayal." They may have been only the most straightforward expressions of his own predicament—between hard times and his broken family situation, there wasn't much left for Willie and his sister—but it was obvious even then that Willie meant his songs as more than a momentary plaint. As he remembers it, by the age of five he had already begun to write poetry; a year later he learned to play guitar; before long he had married the two callings, becoming, in his own words, "a serious songwriter by the age of eight." Three years later, he had enough songs to compile his own homemade songbook.

Willie started playing guitar with a German band

led by John Raycheck when he was about twelve; dish-
ing out the polkas, Schottisches and waltzes taught
him that music was about dancing and having a good
time—a lesson reinforced by the Western Swing that
ruled Texas in his youth. When he was eighteen, after
a stint in the Air Force, he married sixteen-year-old
Martha Mathews, and for some time the couple moved
from place to place around the country—to Vancou-
ver, Washington (where his mother lived); to San Antonio; to Fort Worth. Working as a disc jockey during
the week, he performed on weekends, putting his
teenage experience to work while he dreamed of becoming a part of the greater world of country music.
In 1957, Willie cut his first record, the self-penned
"No Place For Me," with the Leon Payne song "The
Lumberjack" on the flip side. He paid for the recording session himself, and even footed the bill to
press the record; the label said it all: "Willie Nelson
Records." He promoted it wherever he went.

He had his eye on bigger things—Nashville, eventually—but he set up temporarily in Pasadena, Texas,
just outside Houston, where he landed a job as a disc
jockey and guitar teacher, and set out trying to hawk
his songs.

Nashville publishers generally say it takes three to
five years after a songwriter moves to Nashville before
he or she can make a go of professional songwriting,
because as much as they're imbued with the "art" of
country writing, they can't get anywhere before they
learn the "craft." But even in his Texas days Willie
had crafted a batch of first-class songs; he just had no
immediate way of knowing whether they'd work in
Nashville—until he began offering to sell them out-
right. Desperate for money to support his wife and,
by now, three small children, he offered a local singer,
Larry Butler, the rights to "Mr. Record Man" for $10;
Butler wouldn't buy the song, but sent him $50. He
sold Paul Buskirk, who employed him at the Paul
Buskirk School of Guitar, the song "Family Bible" for

another $50, and "Night Life" for a whopping $150. Buskirk got another Texan, Claude Gray ("The Tall Texan") to record "Family Bible" on Houston's Big D Records; the song debuted on the national charts in March, 1960, and eventually reached the No. 10 position.

Though he'd never see royalties from the songs, Nelson says he never regretted selling them to Buskirk, because he "needed money in a big way" when he'd sold them. "I appreciate that Paul and his partners knew a bargain when they saw it." Buskirk's partner, Walt Breelin, is officially listed as a co-writer on "Family Bible," as is Claude Gray, who got partial songwriting credit in exchange for recording the song.

The man who owned Big D Records, Pappy Dailey, was George Jones's manager; after Dailey turned down the chance to take on Willie's song "Night Life," Nelson went into the studio to record it himself; released on another self-financed label under the name "Hugh Nelson," it didn't get any further than "No Place For Me." But Buskirk had shown faith in the songs—faith enough to buy them, anyway—and that was good enough for Willie: Their success "encouraged me to think I could write a lot more songs that were just as good."

As he put it in his autobiography, Willie Nelson moved to Nashville from Houston in 1960 because "Nashville was where the store was. If I had anything to sell, it must be taken to the store. . . . I knew if I was going to be recognized widely I would have to make it in Nashville." If he had already, in some small way, begun to "make it" on the strength of "Family Bible" and "Night Life" (Willie's self-financed record of the latter earned him a little attention in Music City, and in 1963 it would become a hit for Ray Price), he was right nevertheless: He had to get there to go all the way. When Nelson arrived, he started hanging out at a place just across the alley from the Grand Ole Opry called Mom's, which would become the famous

Tootsie's Orchid Lounge a little while later. Downtown Nashville was still the center of the country music industry back then; though Owen Bradley and Jim Denny were set up on 16th Avenue, S, and Music Row was setting down roots, country's power structure was still down with the WSM offices, the Ryman Auditorium (where the Opry was held each week), the Ernest Tubb Record Shop and Tree Publishing on 7th Avenue.

Willie soon hooked up with songwriter Hank Cochran, who was working for Pamper Music as a staff writer and "plugger," taking songs to artists and producers and trying to convince them to record them. Cochran, from Isola, Mississippi, was two years older than Nelson, and had moved to Nashville the year before after appearing on the California Hayride. Hank and Willie struck up an immediate friendship; recognizing Nelson's talent, Cochran took him to see Hal Smith, co-owner of Pamper. Smith liked Willie's songs, but couldn't pay him; later, Cochran offered to take the $50-a-week raise he'd just been given and donate that to Nelson as a draw against future royalties, giving Nelson a weekly income. When Cochran went out to Nelson's trailer-home on Dickerson Road and told him he had a job writing songs for Pamper, Nelson recalls, "I broke down and cried."

It was a bonanza for Pamper, too. Cochran and Nelson clicked quickly: The next year, 1961, saw Patsy Cline hit with a new song from Hank ("I Fall to Pieces"), and one from Willie: "Crazy."

Recording Begins

A happy result of his songwriting success came when Nelson landed a recording contract with Liberty Records; his first single was another of his own songs, "Touch Me," which debuted in May, 1962, and reached No. 7 on the country charts. His first album for Liberty, *And Then I Wrote*, contained twelve songs—and he wrote them all. It began with "Touch Me," a song about "someone who's lost everything he can lose," and jumped right on to "Wake Me When It's Over," another song of utter loss: The singer retreats to sleep "till the blues get up and leave my bed." "Hello Walls" finds the singer gone mad through loneliness—and "Crazy," the song Patsy Cline made famous, finds him mad merely for love. "Funny How Time Slips Away," one of country's most famously caustic songs, sketches a scene of strained confrontation between old and new lovers of the same woman. And "The Part Where I Cry" carries on another great country-lyric tradition: The metaphor song. Life and love are a movie: "My biggest line was goodbye."

The album continued with "Mr. Record Man"—a standard play-my-song song—but "Three Days" hints at Nelson's deeper pain: his three dark days are yesterday, today, and tomorrow. After "Undo the Right," another song of confrontation, Nelson sounds one of the definitive notes of his early lyric writing: "Darkness on the Face of the Earth," as bleak an image as exists in the shadowy country universe. The album ends with "Where My House Lives," which brings things down again to human scale and introduces the image that would dominate so much of Willie's early writing: The empty home.

But despite the consistent quality of his first album, the 1960s were not green pastures for Willie Nelson the recording artist; it was his songwriting that carried him along. He released a string of singles—"Half a Man" in 1963, "You Took My Happy Away" in 1964—and then signed with RCA in 1965, where the singles continued through 1971: "She's Not For You," "I Just Can't Let You Say Goodbye," "One in a Row," "The Party's Over," "Blackjack County Chain," "San Antonio," "Little Things," "Good Times," "Johnny One Time," "Bring Me Sunshine," "I Hope So," "Once More With Feeling," "Laying My Burdens Down,"

"I'm a Memory," "Yesterday's Wine." But the highest any of these reached was No. 13.

Years later Willie would look back at his recordings for RCA and feel frustration, especially at the string-laden sound that sweetened his stark, sparse delivery. But at that time RCA was making millions of dollars with lush ballads from the likes of Jim Reeves and Eddy Arnold, and Nelson himself knew he hadn't been reluctant at the time to try on the trappings of country-pop; the label executives had found a successful formula, and it wasn't until later—when he found the sound that *was* right for him—that he came to see what had been wrong with the sixties singles.

The 1960s saw the breakup of one marriage and the beginning of another for Willie Nelson; they saw him form a band, only to quit the performing end of the business altogether to retreat into a life of raising hogs and writing songs. They saw him plunge back into performing again a little later, only to have trouble finding an audience. They saw his maturation as a songwriter.

All these changes in Nelson's life came just as country itself was nearing a cultural crossroads. During the socially turbulent sixties, the country music audience seemed to remain one of the few dependably conservative bastions: As the rest of the country grew their hair and turned to Britain for inspiration, the profile of the country fan matched that of Richard Nixon's "Silent Majority" (preferring Alabama Governor George Wallace to Nixon in 1968, but Nixon to Hubert Humphrey). But even within country fissures began to show, splits of all kinds from the norms of the post-war era: Nascent feminism showed in songs like Loretta Lynn's "Fist City" and Tammy Wynette's "I Don't Wanna Play House"; a bit of social hypocrisy was exposed by Jeannie C. Riley in "Harper Valley P.T.A."; country even found integration in the person of Charley Pride. Perhaps most telling was the fascinating career of Merle Haggard, who became a voice of the rebel South with songs like "Okie From Muskogee" and "Fightin' Side of Me," while at the same time standing for prison reform by refuting the traditional conservative claim that the only way to solve crime was to lock up the criminals and throw away the key.

Willie Nelson may have been the most visible personification of all these seismic shifts. Publicity photos from the early sixties show him at the height of respectability: close-cropped hair, British tailoring, no grizzle at all. But when Nelson (after some initial reluctance) openly embraced Charley Pride in Dallas, it helped pave the way for Pride's acceptance by the honky-tonk crowd; and, as the sixties progressed, Nelson began turning away from the lifestyle and vices of the establishment—booze and cigarettes among them—to embrace the counterculture and its drug of choice, marijuana. His hair grew long; the three-button suits became jeans; he pierced his ear. Always a free spirit in his private life, now he let it show in public.

Still, Nashville wasn't the easiest place to break with tradition, either personally or professionally. It wasn't until his Nashville home burned down in 1971 that Willie made the choice to move back to Texas—and put his career where he wanted it.

Nashville Versus Texas

A true Texan isn't truly happy anywhere else. Given the choice and the chance, he believes, anyone of sound mind would rather live in Texas. And should a true Texan manage to land outside his home state, all he does is count the days until he can get back again. Willie Nelson is a true Texan.

Texas (and, yes, Oklahoma) are where the heart and spirit of country music live. From the cowboys driving cattle north to the Kansas railheads in the 1860s, to the Singing Cowboy, Gene Autry, of the 1930s; from the founders of Western Swing—Bob Wills, Milton Brown, W. Lee O'Daniel—to honky-tonkers like Ernest Tubb and Floyd Tillman, Texas is where the great movements have had their start. Texas partisans can list their achievements till their own cows come home: the first country record ever made (by Texas fiddler Uncle Eck Robertson); the first country hit (by Texan Vernon Dalhart); the first radio barn dance (over WBAP, Fort Worth). Texas names fill the Hall of Fame: Wills, Autry, Tillman, Tubb, Tex Ritter, Jim Reeves, Hank Thompson. Even the pioneers of commercial country, Jimmie Rodgers and the Carter Family, had strong Texas ties. And it's said that Dallas might have become the recording center of country music if studio wizard Jim Beck hadn't died early.

But Nashville, in Tennessee, is the city that has become synonymous with country, because Nashville controls the business side of the industry. The top studios are there; they attract top engineers and musicians; and thus most of the recording of country music is done there. The only thing about country that's beyond Nashville's control is the *creative* side: Genius comes to Music City, often fully formed, and if it makes the proper marriage with the business side it can meet with fame and riches.

As the 1970s opened, Willie Nelson was in a unique position: He was a native Texan, his teeth cut in all the right honky tonks, who'd spent enough time in Nashville—about twelve years—to know all about the industry side of things. So when he moved back to Texas, he had the best of both worlds: He knew his music, and he knew how to get it made.

The Music

Like most people born after 1920, Willie Nelson had his musical tastes formed while listening to the radio. The radio of Willie's childhood carried everything from the Opry, with its established stars, to the celebrities of Texas. Merle Travis, Red Foley, Eddy Arnold, Hank Williams, Webb Pierce, and Lefty Frizzell all had hits as the '40s became the '50s, and even the sounds of Sinatra, Jo Stafford, and the big bands drifted down from the north. But it was Western Swing that ruled the Lone Star airwaves from 1945 to 1955, and it was Bob Wills—Nelson's great influence—who ruled Western Swing.

In Nashville, audiences sit down to listen to their music; in Texas, as Willie had learned with the John Raycheck Band, they get up and dance. From Bob Wills, the leader of the Texas Playboys and one of the most raucous and influential American musicians ever, Willie learned his most valuable lessons about performing. "I learned from him to keep the people moving and dancing"—Wills would play four hours without a break—"That way, you don't lose their attention, plus your amplifiers drown out whatever the drunks might yell. The more you keep the music going, the smoother the evening will be." Wills was thrilled by the sounds of Benny Goodman, Count Basie, and the Dorsey Brothers, and the sound that came out of his big band was an amalgam of their horn harmonies and the stomping fiddle music his players had grown up playing; it was the sound of the Texas Playboys that gave Willie Nelson's songs their musical form.

As a lyricist, though, Willie had many and varied role models. In 1960, the year he arrived in Nashville, four very different songs hit No. 1 on the country charts: "He'll Have To Go," a lush ballad by Jim Reeves; "Please Help Me, I'm Falling," a honky-tonk number by Hank Locklin; "Alabam," Cowboy Copas's traditional blues-based song, and "Wings of a Dove," a gospel/rock 'n' roll–flavored cut by Ferlin Husky. The following year, number-one artists included Johnny Horton, Marty Robbins, Kitty Wells, Patsy Cline, George Jones, Jimmy Dean, Leroy Van Dyke, and Faron Young—each a performer with a discernably different style, each a potential performer for Willie Nelson songs.

For Nelson it was frustrating: Should he write to his Texas honky-tonk heritage? Write Texas stomps people could dance to? Try a more sophisticated approach, that might get him somewhere with pop- or jazz-influenced singers like Reeves or Cline? "For a while my songwriting career became a matter of arguing that I wasn't this and I wasn't that—so what the hell was I?" he has recalled. "They couldn't define the songs I was writing, and I was too stubborn to tailor my stuff for the country music market." Country itself, after all, was having trouble keeping its identity clear. Willie even ran into trouble recording demos for singers to use in judging potential new songs: His idiosyncratic singing style, which helped him get across, confused music-industry mavens. "I could sing on the beat if I wanted to, but I could put more emotion in the lyrics if I phrased in a more conversational, relaxed way. . . . [But] people who really didn't know much about music lost the beat in their own minds, so they thought I was breaking meter." It was a classic case of a songwriter trying to please two masters: the song market, and himself. So he wrote, and he sang the songs on the beat.

The Songs

If there is a defining message in the lyrics of Willie Nelson's Nashville-period songs, it is a traditional country-music message: sadness and despair, a hopelessness that any happiness can be found in this life, and a longing for a past when times were better or love was new. If this reflected the turmoil of Nelson's own life—his childhood heartbreak, turbulent marriages and affairs, short-term joy broken by long-term misery—it just as surely fit the image of the tortured, troubled songwriter perfected by Hank Williams. By the time Willie came along, it was an image fully ingrained into the country songwriter's mindset.

But even the earliest songs show a side of Willie that was new to country music's personality profile: Willie was a survivor. The stories he tells are ones of lost love and loneliness, but through it all he conveys an optimism that makes us believe he'll get through it all. In its darker moments that optimism takes the form of pure-grit determination: Romanticism never swallows up realism in Nelson's work, as again and again he faces the cold facts, and stares them down. "Hello Walls," the big hit he wrote for Faron Young, has him literally addressing not just walls but ceiling, window, and anything else he can cast an eye to: "Don't you miss her?" he asks. But it's that steely resolve that carries him through. "We all must pull together," he says, "she'll be gone a long, long time."

These early songs are as striking musically as they are lyrically—"Night Life," "Crazy," "Touch Me," and "Funny How Time Slips Away" all share elements of jazz and blues in their structure and phrasing—and that rhythmic bluesiness makes something new of the lyrics as well. The lines of dialogue that make up "Funny How Time Slips Away" were a fascinating mix of despair and a kind of grimly joyful revenge: The singer clearly relishes the telling of both sides of the tale ("Hello there. My, it's been a long, long time. How'm I doin'? Oh, I guess that I'm doing fine") as it approaches the dark eventual end. "But just remember," Willie Nelson has his singer croon, "what I tell you—in time you're gonna pay. . . . And it's surprising how time slips away." It's the survival instinct, all right, but surviving with a bitter laugh.

With "Touch Me," from 1961, Nelson relies on the old songwriter's clever-turn-of-phrase approach in a more sophisticated way than others had, asking the listener to touch him physically, and then emotionally so "you'll know how you feel with the blues." "Half a Man" puts a stark spin on another double entendre, making his pained singer into a palpably crippled emotional victim. He's come a long way from the old Ernest Tubb lyric, "I've got half a mind to leave you, but only half a heart to go," bringing his listeners with him to a less witty—and truer—portrait of pain.

But one of the most persistent themes in these early songs—not surprisingly, given Willie's own life—was the idea of home. In "Where My House Lives," he tells the story of a man who doesn't have time to go home and be with his love; when she takes off too, leaving only the house that "lives" there, suddenly a strange image becomes an emblem of the toll of the American fast life. It's the empty house that's the prevalent image here: "Lonely Little Mansion" tells of a house for sale, "furnished with everything but love," with carpets spotted with tears and a torn photograph tossed on the floor. In "She's Still Gone," written with second wife Shirley Collie, he wakes up in an empty house and realizes he's still alone. The narrator of "I Just Dropped By" returns to the home where he and his wife used to live, staring at the door "where she used to stand . . . and wait for me to come home every night." But the crush of suburban proximity drives him away: "The neighbors like to pry. . . . Someone just might not understand." Most telling is "Home Motel"—home as just a place to stay from time to time, "a crumbling last resort when day is through."

It isn't until later in his career—until he leaves Nashville, more or less—that full-blown joy emerges in Willie Nelson's songs. More often, the lighter side of Willie Nelson's early lyrics comes in his moments of wry humor: "I Gotta Get Drunk"'s fatalistic humor (when the doctor tells him to "start slowin' it down," he retorts, "there's more old drunks than there are old doctors"); the whimsical renunciation of "I Can

Get Off On You"; the country-song-on-its-head play of the "Good Hearted Woman" and the "good-timin' man" who loves her.

But to look only at individual songs in the halcyon days of Willie Nelson's songwriting career is to ignore one of the most important facets of his career: his music as it was presented in a series of "concept albums" that forever cemented his image in America's mind.

The Concept Albums

Four of the major milestones of Willie Nelson's career are the four concept albums that mark his turning points—the first when he was suffering frustrations as an artist; the second as he was finding his artistic voice; the third his breakthrough commercial success; the fourth at his superstar height.

His first concept took the form of *Yesterday's Wine*, recorded in Nashville and released in 1971, and chronicles a man's complete life cycle. The album begins with Willie's spoken dialogue, with its direct question, "Do you know why you're here?" Willie mixes Christianity and astrology in his quest, acknowledging "Perfect Man" and then the "imperfect man," a Taurus, "born under the same sign twice." It's a message album, clearly: The first song, a medley of "Where's the Show" and "Let Me Be a Man," is deeply spiritual; its opening words, the plaint to God "Can you use me?", emblematize the directness that was swiftly becoming a Nelson trademark.

"In God's Eyes" comes in next like a sharp point of light, incisive yet gentle. A characterization of God's view of man (at least from the singer's perspective), it warns others not to "think evil thoughts," to "lend a hand . . . to a stranger," then concludes with the biblical image of sheep who go astray and the lesson of the Prodigal Son: "Open arms should await its returning." The album also revives one of Willie's earliest songs, "Family Bible," a song of nostalgia that heralds a simpler time in the singer's life even as it embraces—and evangelizes—his Christian heritage.

"It's Not for Me to Understand" asks questions with no answer, and leaves trouble in its wake. The singer sees a young blind boy, and wonders to God about his plight; as the Lord responds, "it's not for you to understand." "You too are blind without my eyes," God reminds him, overwhelming the singer with the shadow of his shortcomings. After the brief "These Are Difficult Times," and the plea for optimism, "Remember the Good Times," side two opens with one of the signal songs of the disc, "Summer of Roses."

A love song about the temporality of both love and life on earth, "Summer of Roses" crystallizes the album's message—that man is but a fleeting presence, just a speck in God's universe. "December" nods to the end of the year and the end of a relationship, another gesture toward the cycles of life. The title song finds the singer sharing memories—"yesterday's wine"—with an old love in a barroom; this look back is followed by the more joyful "Me and Paul," its tribute to his friendship with drummer and traveling companion Paul English like a breath of fresh air. "Goin' Home," the close of the album, also closes the cycle: The singer gazes down from above to remember old friends (with comments along the way), in an image that can also be read as a man's return to his (earthly) home and looking forward to re-encountering his past.

The next concept album came several years later. *Phases and Stages* was recorded in Muscle Shoals, Alabama, as part of his multi-album deal with Atlantic. In the liner notes, Nelson characterizes his voices over the course of the album: The first side is sung from the woman's point of view, the second the man's. The theme song—"Phases and stages/circles and cycles/ scenes that we've all seen before/let me tell you more"—segues into "Washing the Dishes," the mournful song of a woman "learning to hate all the things that she once loved to do" as her love comes to an end. The song's close, "someday she'll just walk away," leads directly into "Walkin'," an anguished look at the doomed relationship: "Walking is better than running away, and crawling ain't no good at all." "Pretend I Never Happened" finds the singer taking the blame with one of the harsher lines in Willie's canon: "You will not want to remember any love as cold as mine." But the darkness is halted by two joyously up-tempo songs, "Sister's Coming Home" (about a woman who has returned home from a failed relationship) and "Down at the Corner Beer Joint" (in which she goes out and dances her troubles away). The wistful "(How Will I Know) I'm Falling In Love Again" offers a ray of hope only to cloud it with doubt: As questions fill the air and the heart, the woman wonders if she's making another mistake, whether she'll "lose or win."

Side Two's "Bloody Mary Morning" greets a day of reckoning for the male half of this tennis match: It's a love-left-behind song seen through hangover glasses and a series of airplane windows. The sequence of songs that follows—"No Love Around," "I Still Can't Believe You're Gone," "It's Not Supposed to Be That Way," "Heaven and Hell"—find his mind reeling through hurt, disbelief, and broken idealism. "Heaven is laying in my sweet baby's arms," Willie sings, "and Hell is when baby's not there." After a brief reprise of the theme, *Phases and Stages* surges toward its close with "Pick Up the Tempo," a freedom cry: Willie won't let anyone else run his life, he'll just "pick up the tempo just a little and take it on home."

Phases and Stages represents a "sensitive" attempt at relationship-portraiture that ends up being a re-statement of the old double standard: It's the man who's been unfaithful, the woman who keeps the home fires burning. If, in Willie's always forward-looking vision, the woman's future seems to hold new love, for the man it holds a different kind of promise: That of living life to the fullest, of making a combined declaration of freedom and career decision to follow his own path.

Red Headed Stranger, from 1975, became Willie Nelson's third concept album, and it was also his commercial breakthrough; recorded as his first release for Columbia, it yielded his first No. 1 single, the old Fred Rose song "Blue Eyes Crying in the Rain," and finally made him a superstar at the age of forty-two. The album itself broke new ground; CBS at first balked at the production, which to their sophisticated ears sounded like demos for someone else's record, but Willie's simple approach won the day. And at the same time the album broke, Willie finally found himself reaping the harvest of fellow-feeling he had sown during his years in Nashville: His years as a songwriter's songwriter, combined with his ever-growing circle of influential friends, finally bore fruit. But it was in Texas, again, that the real Willie Nelson groundswell boomed: He began a tradition of Fourth of July picnics in Dripping Spring, Texas, in 1973, that soon made him a cult figure in the Austin "outlaw" scene. His albums for Atlantic had already been noticed by everyone in the country-music world; the buzz was clear—with the right hit single Willie could break out.

There was a zing of irony, then, about the fact that Willie's breakthrough hit, "Blue Eyes Crying in the Rain," wasn't a Willie Nelson original; furthermore, a number of songs on the new album—including the title song, C. Stutz and E. Lindeman's 1953 "Red Headed Stranger"—were other writer's songs, most not very well known, some nearly thirty years old. But the real eye-opening effect of *Red Headed Stranger* was in its hard-country style: It was a backlash against the overproduced studio sounds that had flooded forth from Nashville in the preceding ten years. It's a cyclical phenomenon, the rediscovery of traditional country, almost inevitably followed by its "sweetening" as producers and record companies pine for crossover success. When the single "Red Headed Stranger" was released in 1975, the song it replaced at No. 1 was "Daydreams About Night Things" by Ronnie Milsap; two weeks later Nelson was replaced by Charley Pride with "Hope You're Feelin' Me (Like I'm Feelin' You"). Both were high-gloss production numbers, with country's version of Phil Spector's wall of sound. The sparse instrumentation of Willie's record was almost a relief; it was different, it fit Willie's voice perfectly, and it was purely country.

But the overarching story in this concept album was purely Willie, and the original Nelson songs it boasts were a significant contribution to his work. The album begins with "Time of the Preacher," which outlines the tale: the story of a man who "went out of his mind" when his lover leaves, suffering an emotional breakdown ("he cried like a baby, he screamed like a panther"), mounting his horse, riding out into the world. The suite of songs Willie strings together on side one to fill out the emotional contours of the piece testify to his understanding of good old country music: "I Couldn't Believe It Was True," by Eddy Arnold and Wally Fowler; "Blue Rock Montana"; "Red Headed Stranger"; "Blue Eyes"; and "Just As I Am," the old gospel song, introducing not death but an altar call— for the redemption of the red-headed stranger.

Side two begins with "Denver," Willie's own song, and the city the stranger rides into; he ends up in a tavern, dancing the evening away with a new woman to the instrumental strains of the waltz "O'er the Waves" and old country-dance favorite "Down Yonder." The titles of the songs, again, tell the story: Hank Cochran's "Can I Sleep In Your Arms Tonight," T. Texas Tyler's "Remember Me," and "Hands on the Wheel," in which the stranger is redeemed by a woman's love, pulling his life back together for him. It begins philosophically: The world is "spinning help-lessly out of control," the singer has "no place to go," until he finds "something that's real" in his new lover; "I found myself in you . . . I feel like I'm going home."

Constructed as it is of other people's stories, *Red Headed Stranger* is really like a country song writ large: Just as most country songs are a matter of rearranging and reinventing old country-music images, with this album Willie Nelson rearranged whole country songs into a new, yet wholly authentic, story-song cycle. It's cinematic in feel, and for years Willie tried to get it made into a movie; its story of death and rebirth through a woman's love echoes, among other things, the central Christian story of death and rebirth through love of God. The parallel has its faults: The red-headed stranger's murderous streak is difficult to compare with the image of Christ's death to cleanse man's sins. But the song "Just As I Am" represents a cleansing of the spirit, freeing the stranger to find true love, and this may be the album's message: Even the most imperfect man can find redemption.

Willie's fourth concept album, 1983's *Tougher Than Leather*, returns to a cowboy theme for another story of reincarnation in the Old West. It opens with "My Love for The Rose," and the rose—not just the queen of all flowers, of course, but certainly a Texas image—becomes the central image of the album. "Changing Skies," which follows, finds Willie reflecting again on death and reward, but in a more philosophical light than the harrowing story of *Stranger* allowed: When we die we're not gone, we're just "changing skies." These songs, lyrically no more than vignettes, lead directly into the title song, "Tougher Than Leather," a long story about an old gunfighter who guns down a young cowpoke by getting the youngster to look into the sun. He knows it takes smarts as well as a fast draw to stay alive; but his meanness—he crushes the rose left by the younger man's sweetheart—comes back to haunt him, and he dies from "a poison inside."

And, after another snatch of "Changing Skies," the

message of "old tougher-than-leather" comes to the fore in "Little Old-Fashioned Karma," in which the philosophies of East and West meet: "A little bit of sowing, and a little bit of reaping." Ultimate justice is a concept familiar in both country and the blues, and with the rise of "karma culture" in the '60s and '70s its application to the world of the Old West must have seemed only fitting. Indeed, as the album continues it becomes ever more clearly an expression of Willie Nelson's individualist religious beliefs, mixing fundamentalist Christianity, Zen Buddhism, and mysticism into a law of divine order with heavy emphasis on redemption, justice, and reincarnation.

And yet these images are complicated by other stories within the songs on *Tougher Than Leather*. "Somewhere in Texas Part I" takes up a modern cowboy's wishes to have lived in the Old West; but in "Part II" his life falls victim to a misunderstanding, and through "bad karma" he's sent off to prison for a crime he didn't commit. Longer, echoing "Tougher Than Leather," "The Convict and the Rose" is a cry from the jail cell that man's faulty justice won't prevent the young man from meeting his love in the changing skies. But the album concludes with the ultimate revenge song, "Nobody Slides, My Friend," a companion piece to "Karma" but painfully more direct.

In his autobiography, Nelson writes of his persistent religious sense: "Even as a child I believed I had been born for a purpose, . . . [that] all is one, that every atom in your body was once in a star, that life is continuous and nothing dies, and that the law of Karma—what the scientist would call cause and effect—is as real as electromagnetism." *Tougher Than Leather*, written in 1981 during Willie's recuperation from a collapsed lung, bears all the hallmarks of a longtime fighter confronting his own mortality. And his songwriting, in its use of both traditional and surprising imagery in a freeform structure, was clearly up to the task. From an expertly talented Nashville craftsman, he had become a uniquely expressive and personal songwriter.

Though it came about as a movie soundtrack, there is a fifth collection of songs in Willie Nelson's body of work that might be considered a "concept album": *Songwriter*, written for the movie of the same name, starring Kris Kristofferson and featuring Willie in the role of his manager. The two songs Willie sings on the album, "Songwriter" and "Write Your Own Song," present conflicting attitudes about the lifestyle at the center of the movie—the life Nelson had endured some twenty-five years at that point. "Songwriter," like many of Nelson's songs, is a simple message: "Write it down . . . don't let it slip away . . . someone is listening today." But it's "Write Your Own Song" that comes closer to Willie Nelson's true approach to the world of country music: Let business be damned, he says, we'll "write what we live and live what we write."

The message is that the business side of the music industry can be insensitive, profiting from the sweat and toil of creative folk without showing an ounce of care for them. "We're making you rich/an' you're already lazy," he cries, mincing no words: "Is your head up your ass so far that you can't pull it out?" There's no love lost between writers and the executives hanging over their heads; one gets the feeling that the vehicle of "Songwriter" finally gave Willie Nelson the chance to vent a rage he'd carried with him for a long time.

Back to Texas

With few exceptions, the songs Willie Nelson wrote during his Nashville era (1960–1972) concern love gone wrong. *Shotgun Willie* (1973) and *Phases and Stages* continue the theme. Even *Red Headed Stranger* echoes with it.

But the success of that album was the major reason

Willie Nelson achieved stardom—and, ironically, that stardom, wrought of such painful songs, brought Willie a new outlook on life. Just as other factors contributed to his stardom, Willie's brightened attitude was the result of more than just his new fame: He had moved back to Texas, where he felt more comfortable; he had connected with a powerful musical movement that brought rednecks and hippies together; and he had a happy new marriage. For a long time he had just barely made ends meet, struggling to support a band on tour after tour; after *Red Headed Stranger* his touch turned golden, and money flowed abundant. Record royalties, business ventures (the Fourth of July picnic and a number of Texas clubs among them)—most everything turned out well, infusing Willie with a sense of joy whose expression was his 1979 album *Willie and Family Live*. With that album he returned to his Nashville songs with the fresh confidence of a conquering hero—a man presenting the mementoes of his past as trophies.

If there's a song that marks this crux in Willie Nelson's career, it's "Healing Hands of Time," an old Nashville song of his he resurrected for *The Sound in Your Mind* (1976), the Columbia album that followed *Red Headed Stranger*. It's another song of lost love, but watch the difference: "I've reached mountain peaks and I've just begun to climb," he sings; "I'll get over you by clinging to those healing hands of time."

The move back to Texas, the success that followed, and Willie's newfound creative spark led him in unexpected directions. He made a series of albums celebrating what he thought of as the best of American song, beginning with 1977's Lefty Frizzell tribute *To Lefty from Willie*, and continuing with *Stardust* (1978), produced by Booker T. Jones. *Stardust* was a creative breakthrough, though not for Willie the songwriter: It was a conscious decision to take on what he described as his ten favorite songs—popular standards as well as country songs. Once the struggling songwriter himself, now Nelson had earned enough attention that he could use his place in the public eye to point back to the older masters of his own art— songwriting. It became his biggest-selling album.

As the '70s turned into the '80s, success rolled along: He began appearing in movies, first with Robert Redford in *The Electric Horseman* (1979), then in *Honeysuckle Rose*, his first starring role. When the film's producers asked for a song about the musician's life, Willie took out a piece of paper and wrote "On the Road Again," the words flowing, he wrote in his autobiography, "as if someone else was moving my pen." He wrote it quickly, added music even more swiftly, but it had taken Willie Nelson twenty years on the road to write that song in a few minutes. "The life I love is making music with my friends"—as simple and direct a line as Nelson ever wrote—also captures the essence of the Willie-and-family feeling: Community, spirit, love, hard work . . . and joy.

Nelson has said that in these years he began "consciously trying to find a positive ending to a negative beginning." As he told Rick Mitchell of the *Houston Chronicle* in 1993, "I did a lot of negative thinking in my early years. Like they say, 'A hard head makes a sore ass.'" He quit that thinking, and he quit the drinking that had led to his moody-song-moody-spirit vicious cycle. He still wrote losing-love songs, but now he felt free to write about the brightness of life as well. Moreover, his songs increasingly reached outside his own personal feelings to embrace ideas and issues— his hit "Little Old Fashioned Karma," along with others, represented a new, less insular Willie Nelson.

The 1980s were also a time of playful duets for Willie, who joined with everybody from Julio Iglesias to Ray Charles to Webb Pierce to Leon Russell in song. He became a senior spokesman for country music in these years, and for American music as well; with

Farm Aid, the series of benefit concerts that replaced his Fourth of July picnics, he seemed to become a kind of walking banner of alternative-sensibility patriotism.

It was a good time for Willie Nelson . . . until the 1990s came calling with some bad news. In 1990 the IRS announced that he owed them $16.7 million in back taxes, and seized all his belongings. He had always left his financial affairs in the hands of accountants, but now Internal Revenue had chosen him as the next in their long line of high-profile tax offenders whose punishment serves to strike fear in the wallets of mere mortals. When Willie resolved his differences with the government, part of the settlement involved the release of a spare, acoustic, bill-paying album Willie dubbed *Who'll Buy My Memories: The IRS Tapes*. They couldn't take away his weatherbeaten wit.

The songs on *The IRS Tapes* are Willie's signature songs from the early Nashville days, and it is the quintessential singer/songwriter album, just Willie and Trigger, his ragged acoustic guitar. "Country Willie," "Summer of Roses," "Buddy," "Wake Me When It's Over," "Who'll Buy My Memories": It may be his finest collection.

Today

In 1993 Willie Nelson turned sixty, an event he marked with a CBS TV special and a new album, *Across the Borderline*, produced by rock producer Don Was. Like much he has done in the second half of his career, it seemed to have as one of its goals the celebration of songwriting. Willie sang songs by Paul Simon, Peter Gabriel, Bob Dylan, Lyle Lovett, and Willie Dixon. Many were spiritually a long way from the Texas honky-tonk feel of his own work, yet he took on their deeper messages just as surely as if they were his own: "I live the life I love," he sang in Dixon's classic blues, "and I love the life I live." That, by this point, he could have written himself.

Willie also sang three of his own songs on the album, and co-wrote another, "Heartland," with Bob Dylan. In a unique collaboration, Dylan sent him a tape with the melody—"Duh duh duh da duh *heartland*," sung against chords—and Willie worked up the lyric from that title. The day after his TV special marking thirty years in the business, he went into the studio with Dylan to cut the record.

At sixty, Willie Nelson the songwriter seems to have turned from writing songs of personal trial to crafting lyrics (like "Heartland") that embrace the broader American experience. During the 1980s his vision grew beyond the personal to the universal, as expressed in his own songs and others' he chose to sing, such as "Living in the Promiseland," "City of New Orleans," and "Seven Spanish Angels." Surely his experience as a national voice in connection with Farm Aid had affected him. "There's a home place under fire tonight in the heartland," he sings, bringing a grapes-of-wrath rage and frustration to bear on his song. "There's a big achin' hole in my chest now where my heart was/ And a hole in the sky where God used to be."

"Valentine," also on *Borderline*, was written for Nelson's seventh child, Luke, and it's a triumph of minimalism yet undergirded with the complexity that defines a father's love. "She's Not For You" is an old Nashville Nelson song, from 1962, and it's a classic Nashville lyric of resignation and denial. But "Still Is Still Moving to Me" is the keynote, in which he takes the sentiment of "On the Road Again" and rewrites it as a statement of personal philosophy: "I can be moving or I can be still/But still's still moving to me." The entertainer is always traveling, stopping to entertain as if only to be able to get up and go again. The image is one of the central ones of the American musical tradition, that of the wandering balladeer whose paradox is finding contentment only in constant change of venue—the motto of the rambling man.

In 1994 Willie Nelson returned to Liberty Records,

his first major label, to make a new album, *Healing Hands of Time*, for which he recorded a new song, "There's Worse Things than Being Alone." It offers a snapshot of his mindset in the mid-nineties—"I'm well past halfway in my time/But I still have a lot on my mind."

If life is a golf game, then Willie Nelson may be on the back nine . . . but he's changed the way he plays the game. The seriously dark songs of his early years, wrought from deep personal loneliness, have given way to an outlook that's largely positive: As he told one interviewer, "pure hopelessness is not something I can write about a lot anymore." That odyssey from sadness to hope is the story of Willie Nelson's life, as expressed in the songs he has written, always along with an emphasis on constant movement. Staying in one place is never a troubador's life.

TEXAS

The Early Years

NO PLACE FOR ME

Your love is as cold
As the north wind that blows
And the river that runs to the sea
How can I go on
When your only love is gone
I can see this is no place for me

The light in your eyes is still shining
It shines but it don't shine for me
    It's a story so old
    Another love grown cold
I can see this is no place for me

MR. RECORD MAN

Mr. Record Man, I'm lookin' for
    A song I heard today
There was someone blue who's singin' 'bout
    Someone who went away
Just like me his heart was yearnin'
    For a love that used to be
It's a lonely song about a lonely man like me

I was drivin' down the highway
    With my radio turned on
And the man that I heard singing
    Seemed so blue and all alone
As I listened to his lonely song
    I wondered could it be
Could there somewhere be another lonely man like me

There was something 'bout a love
    That didn't treat him right
And he'd wake from troubled sleep
    And cry her name at night.
Mister Record Man, oh get this record for me
    Won't you please
It's a lonely song about a lonely man like me

FAMILY BIBLE

There's a family Bible on the table
Its pages worn and hard to read
But the family Bible on the table
Will ever be my key to memories

At the end of the day when work was over
And when the evening meal was done
Dad would read to us from the family Bible
And we'd count our many blessings one by one

I can see us sitting 'round the table
When from the family Bible Dad would read
And I can hear my mother softly singing
Rock of Ages, Rock of Ages, cleft for me

Now this old world of ours is filled with trouble
This old world would oh so better be
If we found more Bibles on the table
And mothers singing Rock of Ages, cleft for me

I can see us sitting 'round the table
When from the family Bible Dad would read
And I can hear my mother softly singing
Rock of Ages, Rock of Ages, cleft for me

WHAT A WAY TO LIVE

Each night I make the rounds
To every spot in town
A lonely man with lonely time to kill
What a way to live

The paths my memories take
Just make my poor heart ache
I think of her, I guess I always will
What a way to live

I'd rather lay me down tonight
And never wake again
Than to face another day
The shape my life is in

The jukebox playin' loud
A face among the crowd
So much like hers it makes my heart stand still
What a way to live

THE STORM HAS JUST BEGUN

Each night the ragin' storm clouds
    Take away the moon above
And each day the same clouds
    Take away the sun
My world is filled with darkness
And I'm lost without your love
And I realize the storm has just begun

Can't you see the lightnin' flashing
    Can't you hear the thunder roll
She's gone, she's gone
    The damage has been done
There's a storm within my heart
That keeps me cryin' night and day
And I realize the storm has just begun

The sun was shining brightly
    On the day that we were wed
The day drops made the two of us as one
But since the day you left me,
    Storm clouds gather overhead
And I realize the storm has just begun

I don't want your help or pity
    I don't need your sympathy
All I want is you to be my only one
Another night is coming
    And a long night it will be
And I realize the storm is just begun

MAN WITH THE BLUES

If you need some advice in being lonely
If you need a little help in feeling blue
If you need some advice on how to cry all night
Come to me, I'm the man with the blues

I'm the man with a hundred thousand heartaches
And I've got most every color of the blues
So if you need a little shove in foulin' up in love
Come to me, I'm the man with the blues

I'm the man with a hundred thousand teardrops
And I've got a good selection old and new

If you need some advice in being lonely
If you need a little help in feeling blue
If you need some advice on how to cry all night
Come to me, I'm the man with the blues

MISERY MANSION

Misery mansion
So cold and so grey
You look so lonely
Since she went away

Misery mansion
What secrets you hide
Of a love
That has faded and died

You know all the reasons
Why she said goodbye
And you stand there in silence
While I sit and cry

Misery mansion
Oh, how you've changed
Your walls hold the sorrow
That loneliness brings
A love of a lifetime
Forever is gone
Misery mansion, my home

THE PARTY'S OVER

Turn out the lights, the party's over
They say that all good things must end
Call it a night, the party's over
And tomorrow starts the same old thing again

What a crazy, crazy party
Never seen so many people
Laughing, dancing, look at you, you're having fun
But look at me, I'm almost crying
But that don't keep her love from dying
Misery calls for me, the party's over

Once I had a love undying
I didn't keep it, wasn't trying
Life for me was just one party and then another
I broke her heart so many times
Had to have my party wine
Then one day she said
     "Sweetheart, the party's over"

I'VE GOT A WONDERFUL FUTURE BEHIND ME

Today as I walk through my garden of dreams
I'm alone in the sweet used-to-be
My past and my present are one and the same
And the future holds nothing for me

You say there is happiness waiting for me
But I know this is just fantasy
So I'll trade new tomorrows for old yesterdays
And live in my garden of dreams

Yesterday's kisses still burning
Yesterday's mem'ries still find me
Scenes from the past keep returning
I've got a wonderful future behind me

WHO'LL BUY MY MEMORIES?

A past that's sprinkled with the blues
A few old dreams that I can't use
    Who'll buy my memories
    Of things that used to be?
There were the smiles before the tears
And with the smiles some better years
    Who'll buy my memories
    Of things that used to be?

When I remember how things were
My memories all leave with her
I'd like to start my life anew
But memories just make me blue

A cottage small just built for two
A garden wall with violets blue
    Who'll buy my memories
    Of things that used to be?

RAINY DAY BLUES

Well it's cloudy in the morning
Gonna be raining in the afternoon
I said it's cloudy in the morning
Gonna be raining in the afternoon
And if you don't like this rainy weather
You better pack your bags and move

But if you're running from it, brother
The only road that I can see
If you're running from it, brother
The only road that I can see
Is the road that leads to nowhere
And nowhere is a fool like me

Rain keep a-fallin'
Fallin' on my window pane
Rain keep a-fallin'
Fallin' on my window pane
Never seen so much rainy weather
Guess I'll never see the sun again

Better save those dimes and nickels
Save 'em for a rainy day
You'd better save your dimes and nickels
Save 'em for a rainy day
It ain't gonna keep the rain from coming
But at least you know you've paid your way

NIGHT LIFE

When the evening sun goes down
You will find me hangin' 'round
    The night life
    ain't a good life
    but it's my life

Many people just like me
Dreamin' of old used-to-bes
    The night life
    ain't a good life
    but it's my life

Listen to the blues that they're playin'
Listen to what the blues are sayin'

Mine is just another scene
From the world of broken dreams
    The night life
    ain't a good life
    but it's my life

NASHVILLE

CONGRATULATIONS

I can tell that you're already growing tired of me
    You want no part of me
    Even started lying to me
And if you started out to break this heart inside of me
    Congratulations to you, dear
    You're doin' fine

I pass you on the street and you don't speak to me
    You just look at me
    Then you walk away from me
If you started out to make a fool of me
Congratulations to you, dear, you're doin' fine

Well, you should be commended for
    The sorrow you caused me
    How does it feel to be the queen of misery?
(So) if you started out
    to break this heart inside of me
Congratulations to you, dear
    You're doin' fine

COUNTRY WILLIE

You called me Country Willie
The night you walked away
With the one who promised you a life of joy
You thought my life too simple
And yours was much too gay
To spend it living with a country boy

I'm writing you this letter
I write you every day
I hope that you've received the ones before
But I've heard not one word from you
And every day I pray
That you will not forget your country boy

While you're living in the city
With riches at your door
Is this your love, is this your kind of joy?
Or do you find there's something missing
Does your heart cry out for more?
And do you sometimes miss your country boy?

A cottage in the country
With roses 'round the door
Could not compete with flashing city lights
But it's all I have to offer
Except for one thing more:
A heart so filled with love that it could die

Well, it's time to end this letter
The light of dawn is near
A lonely night has passed
But there'll be more
Just one more thing in closing
For all the world to hear:
Come home, I love you
        Signed, your country boy

CRAZY

Crazy
        crazy for feelin' so lonely
I'm crazy
        crazy for feelin' so blue

I knew
        you'd love me as long as you wanted
And then someday
You'd leave me for somebody new

Worry
        why do I let myself worry?
Wond'rin'
        what in the world did I do?

Crazy
        for thinking that my love could hold you
I'm crazy for tryin'
Crazy for cryin'
And I'm crazy
        for lovin' you

DARKNESS ON THE FACE OF THE EARTH

The morning that you left me
Was just another day
How could I see the sorrow that had found me?
And then you laughed and told me
That I was in your way
And I turned and ran as heaven fell around me

I stumbled through the darkness
My footsteps were unsure
I lived within a world that had no sunshine
When you left me darlin'
My world came to an end
And there was darkness on the face of the earth

The stars fell out of heaven
The moon could not be found
The sun was in a million pieces scattered all around
Why did you ever leave me?
You knew how it would hurt
And now there's darkness on the face of the earth

FUNNY HOW TIME SLIPS AWAY

Hello there
    My it's been a long, long time
How'm I doin'?
    Oh, I guess that I'm doing fine
It's been so long now
But it seems now
    Like it was only yesterday
Gee, ain't it funny
How time slips away?

How's your new love?
    I hope that he's doing fine
I heard you told him
    That you'd love him till the end of time
Now, that's the same thing
    That you told me
    Seems like just the other day
Gee, ain't it funny
How time slips away?

Gotta go now
    I guess I'll see you around
Don't know when though
    Never know when I'll be back in town
But just remember
    What I tell you
    In time, you're gonna pay
And it's surprising
How time slips away

GO AWAY

Go away
Can't you see I'm crying?
Go back to the new love that you've found
    Don't sweet-talk me
'Cause I ain't listening
And you only make things worse
    By hanging around

I know that I'd be crazy
If I took you back again
    But this foolish heart of mine
    Might just weaken and give in

So go away
I feel much better when you're gone
For you're the one who made me cry
    Now let me cry alone

I know that I'd be crazy
If I took you back again
    But this foolish heart of mine
    Might just weaken and give in

So go away
I feel much better when you're gone
For you're the one who made me cry
    Now let me cry alone

HEARTACHES OF A FOOL

Started out with the dreams
    And the plans of a wise man
And ended up with the heartaches of a fool

As a boy, I would walk through the valleys
And gaze at the world all around
Made a vow that somehow
    I would find fame and fortune
Well, I found it, but look at me now

Had a sweetheart who would love me forever
Didn't need her, I would reign all alone
Now look at me, I'm the king of a cold, lonely castle
The queen of my heart is gone

Gather round me you fools for the dollar
Listen to me, a lesson you'll learn
Wealth is happiness and love
    Sent from heaven above
And the fires of ambition will burn

HELLO WALLS

Hello walls
    How'd things go for you today?
Don't you miss her
    Since she up and walked away?
And I'll bet you dread to spend
Another lonely night with me
But, lonely walls, I'll keep you company

Hello window
    Well, I see that you're still here
Aren't you lonely
    Since our darling disappeared?
Well, look here, is that a teardrop
In the corner of your pane?
Now, don't you try to tell me that it's rain

She went away
    And left us all alone
    The way she planned
Guess we'll have to learn to get along
    Without her if we can

Hello ceiling
    I'm gonna stare at you awhile
You know I can't sleep
    So won't you bear with me awhile?
We must all pull together
or else I'll lose my mind
Cause I've got a feelin'
    She'll be gone a long, long time

HOW LONG IS FOREVER?

I fell too hard
    And much too deep in love with you
I let you come and go
    At will it seems
Now you're back again, this time you say
    Forever
And I wonder just how long forever means

How long is forever
    This time?
How long until one night
    You don't come home again?
How long is forever
    This time?
How long until I'm all alone again?

People say I'm foolish
    When I take you back
And it could be they're right
    But who can say?
And you'd be welcome here within my arms
    Forever
Even if forever ends for me today

How long is forever
    This time?
How long until one night
    You don't come home again?
How long is forever
    This time?
How long until I'm all alone again?

I CAN'T FIND THE TIME

I've searched through each moment
    Of each passing hour
But your memories grow stronger I find
Oh, they tell me in time I'll forget you
    But somehow I can't find the time

They tell me in time I'll find another
And happiness again will be mine
Oh, they tell me in time I'll forget you
    But somehow I can't find the time

Something each moment reminds me of you
You always end up on my mind
Oh, they tell me in time I'll forget you
    But somehow I can't find the time

I DIDN'T SLEEP A WINK

Didn't sleep a wink last night
Cause you walked out the night before
Just been sittin' here a-rockin'
Hopin' you'd come knockin', knockin' at my door

Watched the moon pass by my window
The stars faded out of sight
The sun came into view
And still I thought of you
And I didn't sleep a wink last night

Trying to remember what I've done
    To make you treat me so?
What have I been guilty of? I'd just like to know
    Thought if we could talk it over
Maybe I could make things right
'Cause until I'm forgiven
    I'm existing, I'm not livin'
And I didn't sleep a wink last night

LONELY LITTLE MANSION

I'm a lonely little mansion for sale
Furnished with everything but love

I'm looking for someone
    To come live in me
I've got a large picture window
    And a yard filled with trees
The sign reads "two stories"
And that's all that's for sale
But there's so many stories
    I could tell

My windows are closed
And I'm gasping for air
My carpets are spotted
With tear stains here and there
A torn photograph still lies on my floor
And two sweethearts don't live here anymore

I'm a lonely little mansion for sale
And for someone I'd fit just like a glove
I'm a lonely little mansion for sale
Furnished with everything but love

A MOMENT ISN'T VERY LONG

Yesterday as I talked with a friend in town
I forgot to remember that you've gone
For a moment I found myself smiling
    But a moment isn't very long

And last night as I danced with a stranger
And she held her cheek close to my own
For a moment I almost forgot you
    But a moment isn't very long

Every now and then I get a chance to smile
But those every-now-and-thens
    Just last a little while
And tonight I've got a date with a new love
But I know I'd do just as well at home

For a moment maybe I could forget you
    But a moment isn't very long

A NEW WAY TO CRY

All my tears have fallen
I can cry no more
I've cried so much since you have said good-bye
    But I still love you
    As I did before
And I've got to find a new way to cry

The pressure keeps on building up within my heart
It grows and grows but still my eyes are dry
    Though my heart is breaking
    Tears refuse to start
So I've gotta find a new way to cry

I've gotta find a new way to relieve the pain
It just can't stay forever locked inside
    And until I forget you
    And can smile again
I've got to find a new way to cry

I've gotta find a new way to relieve the pain
It just can't stay forever locked inside
    And until I forget you
    And can smile again
I've gotta find a new way to cry

NO TOMORROW IN SIGHT

The children are sleeping
Our talk can begin
We've waited until they've gone to bed
We knew they would cry
When we said goodbye
And I'd rather leave quietly instead

We can never be happy
We both know it's true
We've quarrelled from the day that we met
Our love was too weak
To pull our dreams through
But too strong to let us forget

I hope we can salvage a few memories
To carry us through the long nights
The clock's striking midnight
Yesterday's gone and there's no tomorrow in sight

In our efforts to break through
The thick walls of pride
With harsh words that burned to the core
The walls still remain
But the words broke inside
And strengthened the walls even more

I hope we can salvage a few memories
To carry us through the long nights
The clock's striking midnight
Yesterday's gone and there's no tomorrow in sight

ONE STEP BEYOND

I'm just one step before losing you
And I'm just one step ahead of the blues
But I know that there's been pain and misery
Long before this old world ever heard of me

And I know it will hurt to see you go
But we'll just add one more heartache to the score
And though I still love you as before
I'm just one step beyond carin' anymore

Bet that you're surprised that I could feel this way
After staying home and waiting night and day
For someone who cared so much for me
You'd come home just long enough to laugh at me

I don't know just when my feelings changed
I just know I could never feel the same
And though I still love you as before
I'm just one step beyond carin' anymore

THE PART WHERE I CRY

Life is a picture in which I play the lead
But my biggest line was good-bye
Now my leading lady has walked out on me
And this is the part where I cry

I was great in the scene
    where she found someone new
You should have seen my look of surprise
And if you have just walked into the picture
This is the part where I cry

And after the picture is over
And it's judged for the part she lied
The award of achievement that's given
Will be mine for the part where I cried

SOME OTHER TIME

Some other time I'll forget you
And start my life anew
    But not just now
    I won't forget you
I've spent too much time loving you

I know I could forget you if I wanted to
But there's still a million dreams
That I must dream of you
Some other time I'll stop remembering
The love that came my way
Then I'll forget I ever loved you
Some other time
    But not today

THINGS TO REMEMBER

I've cried so much lately
That I've made out a list
    Of things to remember
    Things to forget
But my mind can't separate
    The joy from regret
I always remember the things to forget

Things to remember
    The day that we met
The day that we parted
    Things to forget

Well, why would my heart
Let me do it this way
With just things to remember today?

Things to remember
    Plans that were set
Plans didn't work out
    Things to forget

TOUCH ME

Touch me
    touch the hand of the man
    who once owned all the world
Touch me
    touch the arms that once held
    all the charms of the world's sweetest girl
Touch me
    maybe someday you may need
    to know how it feels when you lose
So touch me
    then you'll know
    how you feel with the blues

Watch me
    watch the eyes that have seen
    all the heartache and pain in the land
And be thankful
    that you're happy, though standin'
    so close to the world's bluest man
Don't forget me
    take a good look at someone who's lost
    ev'rything he can lose
And touch me
    then you'll know
    How you feel with the blues

UNDO THE RIGHT

If you can't say you love me, say you hate me
And that you regret the times you held me tight
If you can't be mine forever, then forsake me
If you can't undo the wrong
    Undo the right

It was right when you loved me only
But wrong when you held another tight
So before you go away and leave me lonely
If you can't undo the wrong
    Undo the right

It's too late to say your heart is filled with sorrow
You can't undo what's done—why do you try?
So please help me to face the new tomorrows
If you can't undo the wrong
    Undo the right

WAITING TIME

This is the waiting time
I'll wait for you
While you make up your mind
Just what you want to do
They say that things worthwhile
Are worth waiting for
And you're worth so much to me
That I'll wait forevermore

There was a hurting time
I hurt you so
Then came the parting time
I watched you go
But you said perhaps in time
Our love could still be
So this is the waiting time
And I'll just wait and see

WHERE MY HOUSE LIVES

Stop here, across the street to your right
    That's where my house lives
Sometimes I stayed there at night
But mostly I was on the move
Business first, you know
And she'd wait there in her lonely room
But oh, that's been so long ago
    She's gone now
She couldn't stand to be alone
    And now it waits there
This house that used to be my home

I never go there 'cause it holds too many memories
    Since she's gone
But right there is where my house
    lives all alone

ARE YOU SURE?

Look around you
Look down the bar from you
The lonely faces that you see
    Are you sure
      That this is where you want to be?

These are your friends
But are they real friends?
And they love you as much as me?
    Are you sure
      That this is where you want to be?

Please don't let my tears persuade you
    I had hoped I wouldn't cry
But lately teardrops seem a part of me

You seem in such a hurry
    to lead this kind of life
You've caused so many pain and misery

So look around you and take a good look
And just between you and me
    Are you sure
      That this is where you want to be?

THE END OF UNDERSTANDING

Each time you hurt me you say you're sorry
I try to understand and say OK
But there must be an end to understanding
and the end of mine can't be too far away

I try to understand that you're only human
And we all make mistakes every day
But there must be an end to understanding
And I know that I just can't go on this way

Don't you know that love
        and understanding go together?
Ask too much of one and both will die
And there must be an end to understanding
And I know some day I'll reach the end of mine

EVERYTHING BUT YOU

I've got a new car and it drives just like a dream
I've got money and can buy most anything
I've got places to go and things to do
I've got everything, everything but you

I've got a datebook that's just bulging at the seams
I've got the numbers of all the local queens
They give me memories that last a day or two
I've got everything, everything but you

But this new car I drive don't mean anything
Which reminds me, there's a payment overdue
And they say that I'm a man who's got everything
I've got everything, everything but you

FACE OF A FIGHTER

These lines in my face caused from worry
Grow deeper as you walk out of sight
Mine is the face of a fighter
    But my heart has just lost the fight

Round one, you told me you loved me
And I felt my heart falling there and then
The last round you walked off and left me
    And I guess my heart's losing again

Mine is the face of a fighter
I fought for your love with all my might
Mine is the face of a fighter
    But my heart has just lost the fight

THE GHOST

The silence is unusually loud
    Tonight
The strange sound of nothing
    Fills my ears
Then night rushes in
Like a crowd of nights
And the ghost of our old love
    Appears

This strange world of darkness
That comes with the night
Grows darker when it walks my way
And it laughs while I listen
For the breaking of day
And the ghost of our old love goes away

HALF A MAN

If I'd only had one arm to hold you
Better yet, if I'd had none at all
Then I wouldn't have two arms that ached for you
And there'd be one less mem'ry to recall

If I'd only had one ear to listen
To the lies that you told to me
Then I'd more closely resemble
The half a man that you've made of me

If I had been born with but one eye
Then I'd only have one eye that cries
And if half of my heart turned to ashes
Maybe half of my heartaches would die.

If I'd only had one leg to stand on
Then a much truer picture you'd see
For then I'd more closely resemble
The half a man that you've made of me

HAPPINESS LIVES NEXT DOOR

I'm sorry, but you've come to the wrong house
But I know who those flowers are for
The flowers that you have
    Are for someone who's happy
    And happiness lives next door

Someone sends her flowers each evening
And her young heart is flooded with joy
So don't keep her waiting, deliver the flowers
    To happiness who lives next door

The only one who would send flowers to me
Is gone to return no more
But there's some consolation
    To know someone is happy
    And happiness lives next door

HOLD ME TIGHTER

I thought if I could be with you
    Maybe I'd feel better
But I'm afraid I took advantage of your love
I thought if you'd just hold me tight
    Maybe I'd forget her
But I don't suppose as yet
    you've held me tight enough

Please hold me tighter
I still remember
Put your arms around me
Hold me close, hold me tight and long
Please hold me tighter
I still remember
And I can't love again
Until her memory's gone

I thought that surely someone else
    would be the answer
And you're the sweetest answer that I've found
I read somewhere that new love
    Conquers old love
But there can't be new love
    with the old one still around

HOME MOTEL

What used to be my home has changed
    To just a place to stay
A crumbling last resort when day is through
Sometimes between sundown and dawn
Somehow I find my way
    To this home motel
    On Lost Love Avenue

No one seems to really care
If I come here at all
And the one who seems to care the least is you
I'm gonna hang a neon sign
With letters big and blue
    Home Motel
    on Lost Love Avenue

No one seems to really care
    If I come here at all
And the one who seems to care the least is you
I'm gonna hang a neon sign
With letters big and blue
    Home Motel
    on Lost Love Avenue

I JUST STOPPED BY

I just stopped by to see the house I used to live in
  I hope that you don't mind
  I won't stay very long
So long ago someone and I lived here together
And then so suddenly I found myself alone

I couldn't stand the thought
  Of living here without her
And so I moved away to let my memories die
But my memories outlived my own judgment
This may sound strange to you
  But I just thought I'd stop by

The very door you're standing in
  She used to stand there
And wait for me to come home every night
And when I'd see her standing there
  I'd run to meet her
These things were on my mind
  So I just thought I'd stop by

I guess that I should leave
  Someone just might not understand
And I'm aware of how the neighbors like to pry
But you can tell them all today
  A most unhappy man
  Was in the neighborhood
  And he just thought he'd stop by

I'LL STAY AROUND

I'll stay around till it's over
And hope that it never ends
Maybe in time you'll change your mind
     And decide to love me again

I'll just simply refuse to leave you
Call me stubborn but I'll never give in
And I'll just hang around till it's over
     And hope that it never ends

I'll stay around till it's over
And hope that it never ends
Maybe in time you'll change your mind
     And decide to love me again

I'll just simply refuse to leave you
Call me stubborn but I'll never give in
And I'll just hang around till it's over
     And hope that it never ends

KNEEL AT THE FEET OF JESUS

Guess I've been hanging around too long
It's just about time I was moving along
I'm gonna kneel at the feet of Jesus
        In the morning
And don't you worry and don't you moan
It's just about time I was moving along
I'm gonna kneel at the feet of Jesus
        In the morning

I'm gonna kneel at the feet of Jesus
        In the morning
Gonna leave this sinful world
Before the dawning
And don't you worry and don't you moan
It's just about time I was moving on
I'm gonna kneel at the feet of Jesus
        In the morning

And when I'm dead and you carry me away
Don't you bury me deep 'cause I ain't gonna stay
I'm gonna kneel at the feet of Jesus
        In the morning
A little bit of dirt and a little bit of gravel
Don't you weight me down
        'Cause you know I gotta travel
I'm gonna kneel at the feet of Jesus
        In the morning

MEAN OLD GREYHOUND BUS

Mean old Greyhound bus, look what you've done
Took the one I love and away you've run
But you don't have no feelings I can see
Or mean old Greyhound bus you'd bring her back to me

Mean old Greyhound bus, now don't you lie
Didn't the city limits bring teardrops to her eyes
With your big old wheels you pulled our love apart
Mean old Greyhound bus you're out to break my heart

Mean old Greyhound bus, I'm surprised at you
I've never done a single thing to you
But after what you've done I'm mad as I can be
Mean old Greyhound bus please bring her back to me

MY OWN PECULIAR WAY

It would be a comfort to know you never doubt me
Even though I give you cause most ev'ry day
Sometimes I think that you'd
    be better off without me
Although I love you in my own peculiar way

Don't doubt my love if
    sometimes my mind should wander
To a suddenly remembered yesterday
My thoughts could never stay too long away from you
    Because I love you in my own peculiar way

Though I may not always be
    the way you'd have me be
Though my faults may grow in number day by day
Let no one ever say I've ever been untrue
I'll always love you in my own peculiar way

ONCE ALONE

I'm so tired of all this trouble now, aren't you?
We've tried and failed to make our dreams come true
It seems that we had dream worlds all our own
So don't you think that we should try it once alone?

Life's too short to spend it feeling blue
And it's not too late, our dreams could still come true
But before our chance for happiness is gone
Don't you think that we should try it once alone?

It's not your fault and neither is it mine
It seems that we're just victims of the times
It's not that I don't love you cause I do
But love alone can't make a dream come true

I suppose that we'll survive the parting tears
We've survived so many others through the years
But before our chance for happiness is gone
Don't you think that we should try it once alone?

PRETTY PAPER

Crowded streets, busy feet bustle by him
Downtown shoppers, Christmas is nigh
There he sits all alone on the sidewalk
Hoping that you won't pass him by

Should you stop; better not, much too busy
You're in a hurry, my how time does fly
In the distance the ringing of laughter
And in the midst of the laughter he cries

Pretty paper, pretty ribbons of blue
Wrap your presents to your darling from you
Pretty pencils to write "I love you"
Pretty paper, pretty ribbons of blue

PRIDE WINS AGAIN

One time she loved you
And though you still feel the same
Love is always the loser
When pride plays the game

She would never admit she was wrong
And you just couldn't give in
Now you're both a loser
And pride wins again

She would never admit that she was wrong

RIDGETOP

Though part of my heart is with me
Most of my heart must stay
And though I'm three thousand miles from Ridgetop
It's only a memory away

Though I travel to strange, foreign places
There's a memory keeps calling to me
Of hollows and flowers and many happy hours
In Ridgetop in Tennessee

By this time the roses are blooming
The grass in the valleys is green
The wind plays the anthem of Heaven
Through the leaves of the white oak tree

SHE'S NOT FOR YOU

Pay no mind to her
She only wants to play
But she's not for you
She's not for you

And I'm the only one
Who would let her act this way
But she's not for you
She's not for you

So she told you she found heaven
In your eyes
Well I think it only fair to warn you
That sometimes she lies

But it's your heart
I can't tell you what to do
But she's not for you
She's not for you

She just looks for greener pastures
Now and then
And when she grows tired she knows Old Faithful
Will just take her back again

So just leave her here
I'm used to feeling blue
She's not for you
She's not for you

SUFFER IN SILENCE

I think I should speak to you, stranger
    Your problem is clear now to me
You think that the whole world's against you
    And tell everyone that you see

Just suffer in silence
    Speak no bitter words
The world offers no sympathy
Though trouble surrounds you
    And you long to be heard
Just suffer in silence like me

I'll give you a lesson in living
And I hope it stays with you awhile
You're the reason for all of your sorrows
    So suffer in silence and smile

TAKE MY WORD

Take my word for what I tell you
I have never lied to you
Pay no mind to what they're saying
I have never been untrue

Evil tongues in town continue to
Print aloud their evil news
You'll have to take my word when I tell you
    I love you
    I love you
    I love you

The power of gossip is always strengthened
When it finds a receptive ear
If you listen the chances are great
That a thread of doubt may appear

THANKS AGAIN

Thanks for what little love you gave to me
And thank you for my brief escape from misery
And though my short-lived happiness
    Has reached an end
I knew it couldn't last forever
    But thanks again

I'm not sorry for giving all my love to you
And should they ask if I still love you
    I'll have to say I do
    I searched and found a heaven
    And then lost it again
But you were mine for a little while
    So thanks again

My reason for existing is now revealed
I'm just here to show the world
    Just how blue a man can feel
My heart was dead and you
    Made it live and die again
Men may learn from my mistakes
    So thanks again

THERE GOES A MAN

There goes a man
Who gave his heart to someone
    And I feel sorry for him
Cause that someone just gave her heart to me
Now he's the loser and it hurts so much to lose
And I feel sorry for him
    'Cause the loser I know
    Might have been me

Oh, how he loved her
I'm sure he must have loved her
    Almost as much as me

But fate has frowned on him
    Then turned around
    And smiled on me

There goes a man
    Who gave his heart to someone
    And I feel sorry for him
'Cause that someone just gave her heart to me

If things were different
If he had won her love instead of me
I wonder if he'd find the time
    To offer sympathy

There goes a man
    Who gave his heart to someone
    And I feel sorry for him
'Cause that someone just gave her heart to me

THREE DAYS

There are three days I know that I'll be blue
Three days that I'll always dream of you
And it does no good to wish these days would end
'Cause these same three days start over again

Three days that I dread to see arrive
Three days that I hate to be alive
Three days filled with tears and sorrow
        Yesterday, today, and tomorrow

WAKE ME WHEN IT'S OVER

I'm getting tired now
I gotta get some sleep now
I guess I've been worried much too long
And don't wake me till it's over
    When the need for you is gone

I was so happy before I loved you
I want to be like I was before
So don't wake me till it's over
    When I won't want you anymore

My eyes are getting weak now
Gotta get some sleep now
I gotta rest my achin' head
I just wanna lay here
Just let me stay here
    Till the blues get up
    And leave my bed

Good night, darlin'
Good night, darlin'
Good night forevermore
And don't wake me till it's over
    When I won't want you anymore

My eyes are getting weak now
I gotta get some sleep now
I gotta rest my achin' head
Just let me lay here
Let me stay here
    Till the blues get up
    And leave my bed

WITHIN YOUR CROWD

Do you remember
    how they warned you once before?
They made it clear you weren't to see me any more
Within your world of riches
    poor boys aren't allowed
So you must learn to love someone
    within your crowd

Don't you know you're taking chances here with me?
You must protect your reputation, don't you see?
Within your social circle I am not allowed
So you must learn to love someone
    within your crowd

And though I love you more than I can ever say
The danger's much too great and you can't stay
You could never stand dishonor, you're too proud
So you must learn to love someone
    within your crowd

Someday you'll find someone deserving of your love
Someone to kiss the lips that I'm not worthy of
And when I see you passing by, I'll feel so proud
Cause though I stand outside, my heart's
    within your crowd

YOU WOULDN'T CROSS THE STREET
(TO SAY GOODBYE)

Today I stood across the street
And watched you leave with him
Right before my disbelieving eyes
And when you saw me standing there
You turned away from me
And you wouldn't even cross the street
    To say goodbye

Once you said you'd do most anything
    To keep our love
You'd tear out your tongue
    Before you'd tell me lies

Once you said you'd go to any lengths
    To be with me
Today you wouldn't even cross the street
    To say goodbye

Once you said you'd crawl on hands and knees
    To be with me
Today you wouldn't even cross the street
    To say goodbye

I GOTTA GET DRUNK

Well, I gotta get drunk and I sure do dread it
    'Cause I know just what I'm gonna do
I'll start to spend my money
    Callin' everybody honey
    And wind up singin' the blues
I'll spend my whole paycheck on some old wreck
    And brother, I can name you a few
Well, I gotta get drunk and I sure do dread it
    'Cause I know just what I'm gonna do

Well I gotta get drunk, I can't stay sober
    There's a lot of good people in town
Who'd like to hear me holler
    See me spend my dollars
    And I wouldn't think of lettin' 'em down
There's a lot of doctors that tell me
    That I'd better start slowin' it down
But there's more old drunks
    Than there are old doctors
    So I guess we'd better have another round

IT SHOULD BE EASIER NOW

Now that I've made up my mind you're gone
    It should be easier now
Perhaps now my heart will stop hangin' on
    It should be easier now
The lesson I learned from you gold can't buy
A heart can be broken and still survive
Thanks to you now a much wiser man am I
    It should be easier now

The worst now is over, I stood the test
    It should be easier now
They say everything happens for the best
    It should be easier now
The wounds in my heart you've carved deep
    and wide
Hollowed and washed with the tears I cried
But now there will be more room for love inside
    It should be easier now

THE LOCAL MEMORY

The lights go out each evening at eleven
And up and down the block there's not a sound
I close my eyes and search for peaceful slumber
And just then the local memory comes around

Piles of blues against the door
        To make sure sleep don't come no more
She's the hardest workin' memory in this town
Turns out happiness again
        And then lets loneliness back in
And each night the local memory comes around

Each day I say tonight I may escape her
I pretend I'm happy and never even frown
But at night I close my eyes and pray sleep finds me
But again the local memory comes around

Rids the house of all good news
        And then sets out my cryin' shoes
But a faithful memory never lets me down
We're all up till light of day
        Chasing happiness away
And each night the local memory comes around

OPPORTUNITY TO CRY

Just watch the sunrise
On the other side of town
Once more I've waited
    And once more you've let me down
This would be a perfect time for me to die
But I'd like to take this opportunity to cry

You gave your word
Now I'll return it to you
With this suggestion
    As to what you can do
Just exchange the words I love you for good-bye
While I take this opportunity to cry

I'd like to see you but I'm afraid
I don't know wrong from right
And if I saw you would I kiss you
Or want to kick you out of sight?

It's been a long night
So I think I'll go home
And feed my nightmares
    They've been waiting all night long
They'll be the last ones to tell me good-bye
They'll give me many opportunities to cry

PERMANENTLY LONELY

Don't be concerned 'cause it's time I learned
But those who play with fire get burned
But I'll be all right in a little while
But you'll be permanently lonely

And don't be too quick to pity me
Don't salve my heart with sympathy
'Cause I'll be all right in a little while
But you'll be permanently lonely

The world looks on with wonder and pity
 At your kind
'Cause it knows that the future is not very pretty
 For your kind
For your kind will always be running

And wondering what's happened to hearts
That you've broken and left all alone
But we'll be all right in a little while
But you'll be permanently lonely

Running lonely

YOU TOOK MY HAPPY AWAY

When you were with me I was happy
But you took my happy away
You had to go leave me lonely
And my lonely just won't go away

I told you, I told you, I'm sorry
My sorry gets bigger each day
With you in my arms I'd be happy
But you took my happy away

You must know by now how I need you
But you treat my need-you so wrong
You must know by now how I love you
So don't wait till my love-you is gone

ANY OLD ARMS WON'T DO

I'd like to rush into somebody's arms
    And lose myself inside
    But just any old arms won't do
    They must belong to you

I'd like to know the soothing comfort
    Of a love that never dies
    But just any old love won't do
    That love must come from you

I've tried so hard to find someone to love
    Since I lost you
    But they only make me realize
    How much that I need you

I'd like to know when I grow older
    Someone's heart will still be true
    But just any old heart won't do
    It must belong to you

ARE YOU EVER COMING HOME?

Once again it's twelve o'clock and you're still gone
     Honey, are you ever coming home?
I don't mind this waiting for you while you're gone
     But honey, are you ever coming home?

The wind outside is cold as my poor heart inside
     Honey, are you ever coming home?
I love you much too much to worry 'bout my pride
     But honey, are you ever coming home?

Just before I tuck them in
The children question me
     "Why did mommy leave us all alone?"
And I've run out of answers
You've been gone so long
     Honey, are you ever coming home?

BOTH ENDS OF THE CANDLE

I've been trying so hard to forget you
But this chore of forgetting I find
Has me burning both ends of the candle
And fighting a battle with time

What I'd give just to sleep for a moment
But it's a luxury that I can't afford
For I know I would just dream about you
And my tears would start falling once more

So I'm burning both ends of the candle
I just hope that it lasts through the night
For each moment the candle is burning
It brings closer the ending of life

HEALING HANDS OF TIME

They're working while I'm missing you
    Those healing hands of time
And soon they'll be dismissing you
    From this heart of mine
They'll lead me safely through the night
    And I'll follow as though blind
My future tightly clutched within
    Those healing hands of time

They let me close my eyes just then
    Those healing hands of time
And soon they'll let me sleep again
    Those healing hands of time
So already I've reached mountain peaks
    And I've just begun to climb
I'll get over you by clinging to
    Those healing hands of time

I NEVER CARED FOR YOU

I know you won't believe these things I tell you
    No, you won't believe
Your heart has been forewarned
    all men will lie to you
    Your mind cannot conceive

Now all depends on what I say to you
    And on your doubting me
So I've prepared these statements far from truth
    Pay heed and disbelieve

The sun is filled with ice and gives no warmth at all
    The sky was never blue
The stars are raindrops searching for a place to fall
    And I never cared for you

I DON'T UNDERSTAND

I'd be the last one to tell you
    That you shouldn't go
And the first to say be happy if you can
But when you lie and hurt someone
    Who needs and loves you so
Do you mind too much if I don't understand?

I suppose that you're convinced
    This is the thing to do
Life is short and sweet, break all the hearts you can
I guess I shouldn't be surprised
    It's all a game to you
But do you mind too much if I don't understand?

Forgive me but it all seems
    So unreal to me
And my heart and me, we'd made so many plans
But that's all over now
    There's nothing left to do
But do you mind too much if I don't understand?

ONE DAY AT A TIME

I live one day at a time
I dream one dream at a time
Yesterday's dead and tomorrow is blind
And I live one day at a time

Guess that you're surprised to see me back at home
But you know how much I miss you when I'm gone
    And don't ask how long I plan to stay
    It never crossed my mind
I live one day at a time

See that sparrow fly across the cloudy sky
Searching for a patch of sunlight—so am I
    Wish I didn't have to follow
    And perhaps I won't in time
I live one day at a time

SAD SONGS AND WALTZES

I'm writing a song all about you
A true song as real as my tears
    But you've no need to fear it
    For no one will hear it
Cause sad songs and waltzes aren't selling this year

I'll tell all about how you cheated
I'd like for the whole world to hear
    I'd like to get even
    With you cause you're leavin'
But sad songs and waltzes aren't selling this year

It's a good thing that I'm not a star
You don't know how lucky you are
    Though my record may say it
    No one will play it
Cause sad songs and waltzes aren't selling this year

TO MAKE A LONG STORY SHORT, SHE'S GONE

I see nothing to be gained by explanations
No need to try to say who's right or who was wrong
No need to enter into lengthy dissertations
    To make a long story short, she's gone

I won't attempt to explain the things that happened
To put in words why she's not here
    Would take too long
And it's all too far beyond
    The realm of understanding
    To make a long story short, she's gone

The way you look at me
    You don't believe she loved me
But she once loved me
    With a love so sweet and strong
I won't try to give the reasons why I miss her so
    To make a long story short, she's gone

YOU LEFT A LONG, LONG TIME AGO

You tell me today that you're leaving
    But just think a while
    I'm sure that you must know
Today might be the day that you walk away
    But you left me a long, long time ago

Today's just the day that ends it all
    Except the usual mem'ries
    That always linger on
And today might be the day that you walk away
    But you left me a long, long time ago

I stood with helpless hands
And watched me lose your love
    A little more each day
    Then it was gone
And I kept wond'rin'
Just how long until this day would come
Just how long could your pride keep hangin' on

So please don't say you're sorry
    Don't say anything
Don't try to say why you must leave
    Just go
And today might be the day that you walk away
    But you left me a long, long time ago

YOU'LL ALWAYS HAVE SOMEONE

Discontent you must be
Leaving love, leaving me
So go wait for your dreams to come true
    But should young dreams grow old
    And warm friendships grow cold
Someone is waiting for you

If you ever find that fate is unkind
And the devil starts taking his dues
    When your fair-weather friends
    Leave when fair weather ends
Someone is waiting for you

You'll always have someone who loves you
You're never alone, don't you see?
    And when your world's slowing down
    You'll need someone around
Let that someone always be me

AND SO WILL YOU MY LOVE

The music stopped
The crowd is thinning now
One phase of night
Has reached an ending now
But nothing
Nothing lasts forever
Except forever
    And you my love
    And so will you my love

The streets are dark here
While I walk along
And since you've gone
I always walk alone
But nothing
Nothing lasts forever
Except forever
    And you my love
    And so will you my love

The dawn and I
Arrive at home at last
Night turns its lonely face
Toward the past
'Cause nothing lasts forever
Except forever
    And you my love
    And so will you my love

BUDDY

Laugh with me, buddy
Jest with me, buddy
Don't let her get the best of me, buddy
Don't ever let me start feelin' lonely

If I ever needed you, buddy
You know how I really do, buddy
Don't ever let me start feelin' lonely

I cry at the least little thing, buddy
And I'll die if you mention her name, buddy
    Talk to me, buddy
    Stay with me, buddy
Let's don't let her get the best of me, buddy

Let's talk about things as they were, buddy
Before I got mixed up with her, buddy
    Laugh with me, buddy
    Jest with me, buddy
Let's don't let her get the best of me, buddy

I JUST CAN'T LET YOU SAY GOODBYE

I had not planned on seeing you
I was afraid of what I'd do
But pride is strong, here am I
And I just can't let you say goodbye

Please have no fear, you're in no harm
As long as you're here in my arms
But you can't leave so please don't try
But I just can't let you say goodbye

What force behind your evil mind
Can let your lips speak so unkind
To one who loves as much as I
But I just can't let you say goodbye

The flesh around your throat is pale
Indented by my fingernails
Please don't scream and please don't cry
'Cause I just can't let you say goodbye

Your voice is still, it speaks no more
You'll never hurt me anymore
Death is a friend to love and I
'Cause now you'll never say goodbye

SO MUCH TO DO

My oatmeal tastes just like confetti
The coffee is too strong so forget it
The toast is burning, so let it
There's just so much to do since you've gone
    Too much to do all alone

My tie's lost and I can't find my sweater
There's the doorbell, I hope that's your letter
My head aches, I hope I feel better
There's just so much to do since you've gone
    Too much to do all alone

So much to do since you've gone
Too much to do all alone
And time, time rolls on like a river
    And, oh, there's just so much to do
    And I just can't do without you

DID I EVER LOVE YOU?

Did I ever, ever love you?
Did I ever really care?
All the times that I cried for you
Did I really want you there?
Wiser men than I have wondered
About love and never knew
And if I ever loved you
    I guess I still do

All the nights that I spent crying
All those lonely, lonesome times
    Was it my imagination?
    Was it only in my mind?

Wiser men than I have wondered
About love and never knew
And if I ever loved you
    I guess I still do

Is it here today and gone tomorrow?
This love that no one can explain
Can it begin a thing of beauty
Then undergo a dreadful change?

Wiser men than I have wondered
About love and never knew
And if I ever loved you
    I guess I still do

HOME IS WHERE YOU'RE HAPPY

Home is where you're happy
And I'm happy here with you
Or any place on earth that you may be
Home is where you're happy
Just any house will do
And I'll feel at home
    As long as you're with me

This room could not hold me
For one short minute
If you weren't here with me I'd soon be gone
The chair is just a chair
When you're not in it
It takes more than rooms and chairs
    To make a home

Time, someday, may cause this house to crumble
But we'll move into another, love and all
    And if time someday
    Should make your footsteps stumble
I'll be there to catch you should you fall

I LET MY MIND WANDER

I let my mind wander
And what did it do?
It just kept right on going
Until it got back to you

I let my mind wander
Can't trust it one minute
It's worse than a child
Disobeys without conscience
And it's driving me wild
When I let my mind wander

Try to keep my mind busy
On thoughts of today
But invariably memories
Seem to lure it away
My lonely heart wonders
If there'll ever come a day
When I can be happy
But I can't see no way
      'Cause I let my mind wander

THE MESSAGE

I'm writing you this note to say I'm sorry
That's spelled s-o-are you ever coming home?
Can you find it in your heart, dear, to forgive me
That's spelled f-o-how I miss you since you've gone

There are so many things that I want to say tonight
But my mind keeps moving faster
    Than my pen can write

But I hope and pray somehow the message
    Still gets through
That's spelled m-e-s-s-a-gee I love you

ONE IN A ROW

If you can truthfully say
That you've been true just one day
Well, that makes one in a row
        One in a row
        One in a row

And if you can look into my eyes
One time without telling lies
Well, that makes one in a row
        One in a row
        One in a row

Why do I keep loving you?
After all the things you do?
And just one time come into my arms
And be glad that you're in my arms
That will make one in a row
        One in a row
        One in a row

SOMETHING TO THINK ABOUT

You're wondering just what I'll do
Now that it's over and done
Well that's something to think about
And I've already begun

I suppose that I'll find a way
People usually do
But it's something to think about
I'll be lost without you

One thing I would have you do
Please consider the dawn
The dawn of your lonely years
When youth and beauty are gone

And when you can no longer have
Any sweetheart you choose
Here's something to think about
I'll still be thinking of you

TODAY'S GONNA MAKE A
WONDERFUL YESTERDAY

Today's gonna make a wonderful yesterday
One on which I know that I can look back and smile
And with you here with me
    The hours have flown away
And today's gonna make a wonderful yesterday

Today we have made a thousand and one memories
That we can recall when today is a sweet used-to-be
And with you in my arms
    The future seems so far away
And today's gonna make a wonderful yesterday

WHY ARE YOU PICKING ON ME?

You could have your choice of guys around
    Why are you picking on me?
Just snap your fingers, they'll come around
    Why are you picking on me?

I'm well aware of this game
You've learned to love me, then leave me
    And show no concern
And tomorrow you'll have other candles to burn
    So why are you picking on me?

I DON'T FEEL ANYTHING

I don't feel anything
What was I worried for?
I don't feel love or hate
Or anything that I felt before

Why was I so afraid
Of seeing you again?
'Cause it's the strangest thing
I don't feel anything

I must have loved you once upon a time
But I can't seem to feel emotion now of any kind

Why was I so afraid
What this night would bring?
'Cause it's the strangest thing
I don't feel anything

You look the same as always
Time's been good to you
But I must confess that time has done a few things
    For me too

Why was I so afraid
Of seeing you again?
'Cause it's the strangest thing
I don't feel anything

SLOW DOWN OLD WORLD

Slow down, slow down
Old world, there's no hurry
'Cause my life ain't mine anymore
I lived too fast
Now it's too late to worry
    And I'm too blue to cry anymore

I once was a fool for the women
Now I'm just a fool, nothing more
So slow down, slow down
    Old world, there's no hurry
'Cause my life ain't mine anymore

I once had a way with the women
Till one got away with my heart
So slow down, slow down
    Old world there's no hurry
'Cause my life ain't mine anymore

YOU OUGHT TO HEAR ME CRY

If you think I laugh louder than anyone here
If you think that my volume's too high
    If you think I laugh loud
    You ain't heard nothing yet
You ought to hear me cry

I go home to a home where love's almost gone
Not enough to fill one needle's eye
    Then I sit down in a corner
    And I turn on the tears
And you ought to hear me cry

If you think I talk louder than maybe I should
Well, I guess I'm that kind of guy
    But if I talk loud and laugh loud
    You ain't heard it all
You ought to hear me cry

DECEMBER DAY

This looks like a December day
This looks like a time-to-remember day
And I remember a spring
    Such a sweet tender thing
And love's summer college,
Where the green leaves of knowledge
Were waiting to fall with the Fall
And where September wine
    Numbed a measure of time
    Through the tears of October
    Now November's over
And this looks like a December day

This looks like a December day
It looks like we've come to the end of the way
And as my mem'ries race back to
    Love's eager beginning
Reluctant to play with the thoughts of the ending
The ending that won't go away
And as my mem'ries race back to
Love's eager beginning
Reluctant to play with the thoughts of the ending
    The ending that won't go away
And this looks like a December day

GOOD TIMES

When I ran to the store with a penny
And when youth was abundant and plenty
Classify these as good times
    Good times
When I rolled rubber tires in the driveway
Pulled a purse on a string across the highway
Classify these as good times
    Good times

Good times are comin', hummin', hmm
Good times are comin', hummin', hmm

Go to school, fight a war, work steady
Meet a girl, fall in love, for I'm ready
Classify these as good times
    Good times
Here I sit with a drink and a mem'ry
But I'm not cold, I'm not wet, and I'm not hungry
So classify these as good times
    Good times

JIMMY'S ROAD

This is Jimmy's road
Where Jimmy liked to play
And this is Jimmy's grass
Where Jimmy liked to lay around

This is Jimmy's tree
That Jimmy liked to climb
Then Jimmy went to war
And something changed his mind around

This is the battleground
Where Jimmy learned to kill
Now Jimmy has a trade
And Jimmy knows it well—too well
This is Jimmy's grave
Where Jimmy's body lies
And when a soldier falls
Jimmy's body dies—and dies

But this was Jimmy's road
Where Jimmy liked to play
And this is Jimmy's grass
Where Jimmy liked to lay around

LITTLE THINGS

I hope I won't disturb you with this call
I'm just in town for just a little while
And I thought perhaps you'd like to hear the news
Jeannie's grades were the highest in the school

Billy sure does look a lot like you
I understand your other son does too
And Billy said, "Tell Mom I miss her so"
These were some little things
    I thought you'd like to know

Remember Sam and Peg who lived next door?
With them it seemed we always laughed so much
Well Sam and Peg don't live there anymore
I understand they broke up just like us

The house we lived in now has been torn down
Of all the things we owned the last to go
A freeway now runs through that part of town
These were some little things
    That I thought you'd like to know

PAGES

Last evening I turned back
The pages of time
And tore out the chapters
When you were mine

I attempted to cut out
The memories of you
And paste in some new ones
Far better and true
     True

I searched through the chapters
Referring to hearts
For the one with a caption
Till death do us part

I ripped at each letter
And I tore at each word
I screamed at your memory
And nobody heard
     Nobody heard

But your memory's determined
And chances are few
Of my ever finding
A replacement for you
It desperately clings to
The floor of my mind
And fights for its place
     In the pages of time

SHE'S STILL GONE

I wake up in the morning
With my arms around my pillow
Then suddenly I realize I only hold a pillow
    You're not there
    You're not there
I call your name and hear my voice run searching
Through the hallway to return alone, confirming
    All I've known
    For so long
I'm alone
    You're still gone

Still half asleep I stumble
    To the kitchen for my coffee
My footsteps match my heartbeats
    Funny heartbeats on linoleum
    The sounds all wrong
    You're still gone

The sounds outside reminding me
    The world won't wait forever
And understanding saves
    Don't stand by empty graves
    You're on your own
    All alone
    She's still gone

WHO DO I KNOW IN DALLAS?

Who do I know in Dallas?
Who can I call on the phone?
Who do I know in Dallas
That will help me forget that she's gone?

Shirley consoled me in Phoenix
And Jeanie in Old San Antone
But who do I know in Dallas
That will help me forget that I'm alone?

I can't spend the night without someone
The lonelies would drive me insane
So who do I know in Dallas
That will make me be glad I came?

FOLLOW ME AROUND

She always follows me from town to town
At least her memories follow me around
  And whenever I clear my mind
  So she can see
I feel her love come rushing into me

I know that I will never be the law
Looks as though her memory's bound to haunt
  And I know my love
  Will always stay in bounds
Will her memory always follow me around

  Follow me around
  Follow me around
  Follow me around
  Follow me around

And I know my love will always stay in bounds
With her memory always following me around

IT COULD BE SAID THAT WAY

When we look into each other's eyes
Our hearts aren't beating wildly as they beat before
And when we hold each other in our arms
We can't receive the same vibrations anymore

And when we hear each other speak our names
We don't hear the ringing and the singing
        Of a million bells
        Perhaps our hearing's failing us
        Perhaps we're hearing other things
        But who can tell

It could be said that way
It could be said that way
        But I'd much rather say it's time for me to go

What's the point in making leaving any harder
        Than a leaving really ought to be?
And this road on which I travel
Paved with broken glass and gravel
Has just room for me
        I hope there's room for me

I suspect that I'll be lonely
But I know that if I'm lonely
        I'll deserve to be
And I plan to think about you
Just as often as I will
        And that's my plan for me

It could be said that way
It could be said that way
　　　But I'd much rather say it's time for me to go

What's the use in making rhymes
　　　I'd much rather say it's time for me to go

WHAT CAN YOU DO TO ME NOW?

What can you do to me now
That you haven't done to me already?
You broke my pride and made me cry out loud
　　　What can you do to me now?

I'm seeing things that I never thought I'd see
You've opened up the eyes inside of me
How long have you been doing this to me?
I'm seeing sides of me that I can't believe

Someway, somehow, I'll make a man of me
I will build me back the way I used to be
Much stronger now, the second time around
　　　'Cause what can you do to me now?

GOOD-HEARTED WOMAN

A long time forgotten
    Her dreams have just fell by the way
And the good life he promised
    Ain't what she's living today
But she never complains of the bad times
    Or the bad things he's done, Lord
She just talks about the good times they've had
    And all the good times to come

She's a good-hearted woman
    In love with a good-timin' man
And she loves him in spite of his ways
    That she don't understand
Through teardrops and laughter
    They'll pass through this world hand in hand
This good-hearted woman
    In love with a good-timin' man

He likes the night life, the bright lights
    And his good-timin' friends
And when the party's all over
    She'll welcome him back home again
Lord knows she don't understand him
    But she does the best that she can
She's a good-hearted woman
    In love with a good-timin' man

I'M A MEMORY

I'm a game that you used to play
And I'm a plan that you didn't lay so well
And I'm a fire that burns in your mind
    Close your eyes
    I'm a memory

I'm a love that you bought for a song
And I'm a voice on a green telephone
And I'm a day that lasted so long
    Close your eyes
    I'm a memory

I'm a dream that comes in the night
And I'm a face that fades with the light
And I'm a tear that falls out of sight
    Close your eyes
    I'm a memory

Album: *Yesterday's Wine (1971)*

DO YOU KNOW WHY YOU'RE HERE?

Yes, there's great confusion on earth
And the power that is has concluded the following
Perfect man has visited earth already
    and his voice was heard
The voice of imperfect man
    Must now be made manifest
And I have been selected
    As the most likely candidate
Yes, the time is April,
    and therefore you, a Taurus, must go
To be born under the same sign twice adds strength
And this strength, combined with wisdom
    and love, is the key

WHERE'S THE SHOW?/LET ME BE A MAN

Explain to me again, Lord, why I'm here
    I don't know
    I don't know
The setting for the stage is still not clear
    Where's the show?
    Where's the show?
Let it begin, let it begin
    I am born
    Can you use me?

What would you have me do, Lord?
Shall I sing them a song?
    I could tell them about you, Lord
    I could sing of the loves I have known

I'll work in their cotton and corn field
I promise I'll do all I can
    I'll laugh and I'll cry
    I'll live and I'll die

Please, Lord, let me be a man
And I'll give it all that I can
If I'm needed in this distant land
Please, Lord, let me hold to your hand

Dear Lord, let me be a man
And I'll give it all that I can
If I'm needed in this distant land
Please Lord, let me be a man

IN GOD'S EYES

Never think evil thoughts of anyone
It's just as wrong to think as to say
For a thought is but a word that's unspoken
    In God's eyes
    He sees it this way

Lend a hand if you can to a stranger
Never worry if he can't repay
For in time you'll be repaid ten times over
    In God's eyes
    He sees it this way

In God's eyes we're like sheep in a meadow
Now and then a lamb goes astray
And open arms should await its returning
    In God's eyes
    He sees it this way

IT'S NOT FOR ME TO UNDERSTAND

I passed a home the other day
The yard was filled with kids at play
And on the sidewalk of this home
A little boy stood all alone

His smiling face was sweet and kind
But I could see the boy was blind
He listened to the children play
I bowed my head and there I prayed

Dear lord above, why must this be?
And then these words came down to me
After all you're just a man
And it's not for you to understand

It's not for you to reason why
You too are blind without my eyes
So question not what I command
'Cause it's not for you to understand

Now when I pray my prayer is one
I pray His will, not mine, be done
After all I'm just a man
And it's not for me to understand

THESE ARE DIFFICULT TIMES

These are difficult times
These are difficult times
Lord, please give me a sign
For these are difficult times

REMEMBER THE GOOD TIMES

Remember the good times
    They're smaller in number
    And easier to recall
Don't spend too much time on the bad times
    They're staggering and will be
    Heavy as lead on your mind

Don't waste a moment unhappy
    Invaluable moments gone
    With the leakage of time
As we leave on our own separate journeys
    Moving west with the sun
    To a place buried deep within our minds

Remember the good times

SUMMER OF ROSES

A short time I have to be with you my love
But a short time is better than no time you see
So I bring to you all my possessions
And would that you share them with me

I bring you one springtime of robins
One springtime of robins to sing
And I bring you one summer of roses
One summer of roses I bring

I bring you one autumn of dry leaves
Dry leaves will be helpful you know
To soften the fall of your snowflakes
When I bring you your winter of snow

YESTERDAY'S WINE

Miracles appear in the strangest of places
    Fancy meeting you here
The last time I saw you was just out of Houston
    Sit down, let me buy you a beer

Your presence is welcome
    With me and my friend here
    This is a hangout of mine
We come here quite often and listen to music
    Partaking of yesterday's wine

Yesterday's wine
I'm yesterday's wine
    Aging with time
    Like yesterday's wine
Yesterday's wine
We're yesterday's wine
    Aging with time
    Like yesterday's wine

You give the appearance of one widely traveled
    I'll bet you've seen things in your time
So sit down beside me and tell me your story
    If you think you'll like yesterday's wine

ME AND PAUL

It's been rough and rocky travelin'
But I'm finally standin' upright on the ground
After takin' several readings
I'm surprised to find my mind still fairly sound
I guess Nashville was the roughest
But I know I said the same about them all
    We received our education
    In the cities of the nation
    Me and Paul

Almost busted in Laredo
But for reasons that I'd rather not disclose
But if you're stayin' in a motel there and leave
Just don't leave nothin' in your clothes
And at the airport in Milwaukee
They refused to let us board the plane at all
    They said we looked suspicious
    But I believe they like to pick on
    Me and Paul

On a package show in Buffalo
With us and Kitty Wells and Charley Pride
The show was long and we're just sittin' there
And we'd come to play and not just for the ride
Well, we drank a lot of whiskey
So I don't know if we went on that night at all
    I don't think they even missed us
    I guess Buffalo ain't geared for
    Me and Paul

GOIN' HOME

The closer I get to my home, Lord
The more I want to be there
There'll be a gathering of loved ones and friends
And you know I want to be there
There'll be a mixture of teardrops and flowers
    Crying and talking for hours
    About how wild that I was
And if I'd listened to them, I wouldn't be there

Well there's old Charlie Tolk
They threw away the mold when they made him
And Jimmy McCline, looks like the wine's
    Finally laid him
And Billy McGray, I could beat any day
    In a card game
And Bessy McNeil, but her tears are real
    I can see pain
There's a mixture of teardrops and flowers
    Crying and talking for hours
    About how wild that I was
And if I'd listened to them, I wouldn't be there

Lord, thanks for the ride
I got a feeling inside that I know you
And if you see your way, you're welcome to stay
'Cause I'm gonna need you
There's a mixture of teardrops and flowers
    Crying and talking for hours
    About how wild that I was
And if I'd listened to them, I wouldn't be there

LONDON

The streets are dark and quiet
In London after midnight
    Listen
The silence is the master of darkness
And London can sleep tonight
    Protected by the master

London, London
You scream the largest portion of the day
London, London
Rest your lungs, tomorrow's on its way

STAY AWAY FROM LONELY PLACES

Stay away from lonely places
    Follow the crowd
Stay around familiar faces
    Play the music loud
Be seen at all the parties
    Dress yourself in style
Stay away from lonely places
    For a while

Stay away from lonely places
    Till you learn to live alone
Someone's outstretched arms are waiting
    To stay with you at least 'til dawn
Remember that sorrow prospers
    In a heart that never smiles
So stay away from lonely places
    For a while

IF YOU REALLY LOVED ME

If you really loved me
You wouldn't treat me this way
And you'd be kind enough to leave some night
    While I'm away

And I might cry when you go
But I won't die when you go
And someday someone just might come along

And if you really loved me
You wouldn't test me this way
And you wouldn't leave the choice of leaving
    Up to me

But I'm not too proud to survive
'Cause I'm more dead than alive
And someday someone just might come along

THE WORDS DON'T FIT THE PICTURE

If this is a game we play
And if this is a role I play
Where are the words I say to you?
The words don't fit the picture anymore

And if we've been acting all along
  And we both act right
  And we both act wrong
Where does it say that we should cry?
It's just the words don't fit the picture
  Anymore
  Anymore

The words don't fit the picture anymore
No need to force the love scenes anymore
And a one-act play comes to an end
And we turn to leave, we can both part friends
But this is the time to say goodbye
Goodbye, 'cause the words don't fit the picture
  Anymore
  Anymore

MY KIND OF GIRL

My heart takes walks with her
On cold and rainy days
She leads my heart along
Where only love can lead the way
And I know she'll follow me
To the end of the world
She makes me proud to say
That she's my kind of girl

She makes me proud to walk
    The streets of anywhere
And if our bed be grass or cotton she won't care
And I know she'll follow me
    To the end of the world
And she makes me proud to say
    That she's my kind of girl

And I know she'll follow me
    To the end of the world
She makes me proud to say
    That she's my kind of girl

WILL YOU REMEMBER MINE?

Sweet is the song when the song is love
Love that has stood the test of time
And when you've heard all the songs of love
    Will you remember mine?

Gone are the times when I held you close
And pressed your lips to mine
Now when you kiss another's lips
    Will you remember mine?

I have sat beneath the trees
While the cool summer breeze
    Blew away the sands of time
And thought of days when you were near
Remembering when you were mine

Gone are the times when I walked with you
And held your hand in mine
Now when you hold another's hand
    Will you remember mine?

BACK TO TEXAS

SHOTGUN WILLIE

Shotgun Willie
    Sits around in his underwear
Biting on a bullet
    And pulling out all of his hair
Shotgun Willie
    Got all of his family there

Well you can't make a record
    If you ain't got nothing to say
Well you can't make a record
    If you ain't got nothing to say
You can't play music
    If you don't know nothing to play

Now John T. Flores
    Was working for the Ku Klux Klan
At six-foot-five
    John T. was a helluva man
Made a lot of money
    Selling sheets on the family plan

DEVIL IN A SLEEPIN' BAG

We were headed home in Austin
Caught pneumonia on the road
    Taking it home to Connie and the kids
A wheel ran off and jumped a railroad
Then ran through a grocery store
    If you want to buy a bus I'm taking bids

And the devil shivered in his sleeping bag
He said traveling on the road is such a drag
If we can make it home by Friday we can brag
And the devil shivered in his sleeping bag

Well I just got back from New York City
Kris and Rita done it all
    Raw perfection there for all the world to see
Lord I heard an angel singing
In the Philharmonic Hall
    Rita Coolidge, Rita Coolidge cleft for me

WHERE DO YOU STAND?

From somewhere behind you
You've come with your suitcase in hand
Hey, what's your plan?
    Where do you stand?

The world's still divided
And you're still undecided
Decide if you can
Hey, what's your plan
    Where do you stand?

    Where do you stand?
    Where do you stand?
    Hey, what's your plan?
    Where do you stand?

It's time for commitment
It's time for a showing of hands
Hey, what's your plan?
    Where do you stand?

Surely there's someone
    with courage
To say where he stands
Hey, what's your plan?
    Where do you stand?

I'D RATHER YOU DIDN'T LOVE ME

You told me you'd love me forever
But the one in your arms is not me
So if this is what you refer to as love
Then I'd rather you didn't love me

I've waited so long for your love now
But I made up my mind it can't be
For if I am just one of the many you love
Then I'd rather you didn't love me

How can I name the one to blame?
I suppose it's the way you believe
But if this is what you refer to as love
Then I'd rather you didn't love me

Album: *Phases and Stages (1974)*

PHASES AND STAGES

Phases and stages
Circles and cycles
Scenes that we've all seen before
Let me tell you some more

WASHING THE DISHES

Washing the dishes
Scrubbing the floors
    Caring for someone
    Who don't care anymore
Learning to hate all the things
That she once loved to do
    Like washing the shirts
    And never complaining
Except of red stains on the collars
    Ironing and crying
    Crying and ironing
Caring for someone who don't care anymore
Someday she'll just walk away

WALKIN'

After carefully considering
    The whole situation
I stand with my back to the wall
Walkin' is better
    Than running away
And crawling ain't no good at all

And if guilt is the question
    Then truth is the answer
And I've been lying to me all along
There ain't nothing worth saving
    Except for one another
And before you wake up I'll be gone

'Cause after carefully considering
    The whole situation
I stand with my back to the wall
Walkin' is better
    Than running away
And crawling ain't no good at all

PRETEND I NEVER HAPPENED

Pretend I never happened
And erase me from your mind
You will not want to remember
Any love as cold as mine

I'll be leaving in the morning
For a place I hope I find
All the places must be better
Than the ones I leave behind

Well I don't suppose you'll be unhappy
You'll find ways to spend your time
But if you ever think about me
And if I ever cross your mind

Just pretend I never happened
And erase me from your mind
You will not want to remember
Any love as cold as mine

SISTER'S COMING HOME

Sister's coming home
Mama's gonna let us sleep
    The whole day long
    The whole day long
Sister's coming home
Mama's gonna let us sleep the whole day long

Sister's coming home
Mama don't like the man
    Who done her wrong
Sister's coming home
Mama don't like the man who done her wrong

Sister's coming home
Mama's gonna let us sleep
    The whole day long
Sister's coming home
Mama's gonna let us sleep the whole day long

DOWN AT THE CORNER BEER JOINT

Down at the corner beer joint
Dancing to the rock 'n' roll
    Sister likes to do it
    Sister likes to move her soul

Down at the corner beer joint
Dancing on the hardwood floor
    The jeans fit a little bit tighter
    Than they did before

Than they did before
Than they did before
Lord her jeans fit a little bit tighter
Than they did before
Than they did before
Than they did before
Oh the jeans fit a little bit tighter
    Than they did before

(HOW WILL I KNOW)
I'M FALLING IN LOVE AGAIN

I'm falling in love again
I never thought I would again
    I never thought I would

And I may be making a mistake again
But if I lose again
    How will I know?

How will I know?
How will I know?
How will I know?

And I'm falling in love again
And if I lose or win
    How will I know?

BLOODY MARY MORNING

Well it's a bloody mary morning
Baby left me without warning
    Sometime in the night
So I'm flying down to Houston
With forgetting her the nature of my flight

As we taxi toward the runway
With the smog and haze reminding me
    Of how I feel
Just a country boy who's learning
That the pitfalls of the city
    Are extremely real

All the nightlife and parties
Temptation and a seat
    The order of the day
Well it's a bloody mary morning
'Cause I'm leaving baby
    Somewhere in LA

Well our golden jet is airborne
And Flight 50 cuts a path
    Across the morning sky
And a voice comes through the speaker
Reassuring us Flight 50
    Is the way to fly
And a hostess takes our order
Coffee, tea, or something stronger
    To start off the day
Well it's a bloody mary morning
'Cause I'm leaving baby
    Somewhere in LA

NO LOVE AROUND

Well, I come home last Saturday morning
Well, I come home and found you gone
Well, there was a note tacked on my door
Said your baby don't love you anymore

Well, I got dressed up and I went downtown
I got dressed up and I went downtown
And I walked up and I walked down
Well, there weren't no love around

No there weren't no love around
      There weren't no love around
      There weren't no love around
      There weren't no love around

Well, I come home and I lay down
I felt my head spinning round and round
Lord, I poured my dreams and I drank 'em down
No there weren't no love around
      There weren't no love around

I STILL CAN'T BELIEVE YOU'RE GONE

This is the very first day since you left me
But I've tried to put my thoughts in a song
And all I can hear is myself singing
'Cause I still can't believe you're gone

I still can't believe that you'd leave me
    What did I do that was so wrong?
There's just too many unanswered questions
    And I still can't believe you're gone

But you're gone and I'm alone and I'm still living
I don't like it but I'll take it till I'm strong
And all I can hear is myself singing, baby
'Cause I still can't believe you're gone

IT'S NOT SUPPOSED TO BE THAT WAY

It's not supposed to be that way
You're supposed to know that I love you
But it don't matter anyway
If I can't be there to control you
And, like the other little children
You're gonna dream a dream or two
But be careful what you're dreamin'
Or soon your dreams'll be dreamin' you

It's not supposed to be that way
You're supposed to know that I love you
But it don't matter anyway
If I can't be there to console you
And when you go out to play this evenin'
Play with fireflies till they're gone
And then rush to meet your lover
And play with real fire till the dawn

It's not supposed to be that way
You're supposed to know that I love you
But it don't matter anyway
If I can't be there to console you

HEAVEN AND HELL

Well sometimes it's heaven
And sometimes it's hell
    And sometimes I don't even know
Sometimes I take it as far as I can
    And sometimes I don't even go
My front tracks are bound for a cold-water well
And my back tracks are covered with snow
And sometimes it's heaven and sometimes it's hell
    And sometimes I don't even know

Heaven ain't walking on a street paved with gold
Hell ain't a mountain of fire
Heaven is laying in my sweet baby's arms
And Hell is when baby's not there

Well my front tracks are bound for a cold-water well
And my back tracks are covered with snow
And sometimes it's heaven and sometimes it's hell
    And sometimes I don't even know

PICK UP THE TEMPO

People are saying that time will take care
    Of people like me
And that I'm living too fast and they say I can't last
    For much longer
But little they see that their thoughts of me
    Is my savior
And little they know that the beat ought to go
    Just a little faster

So pick up the tempo just a little
    And take it on home
The singer ain't singing
And the drummer's been draggin'
    Too long
Time will take of itself so just leave time alone
And pick up the tempo just a little
    And take it on home

Well I'm wild and mean, I'm creating a scene
    I'm goin' crazy
Well I'm good and bad and I'm happy and sad
    And I'm lazy
I'm quiet and I'm loud and I'm gatherin' a crowd
    And I like gravy
I'm 'bout half off the wall but I learned it all
    In the Navy

Album: *Red-Headed Stranger* *(1975)*

TIME OF THE PREACHER

It was the time of the preacher
When the story began
Of a choice of a lady
And a love of a man
And how he loved her so dearly
He went out of his mind
When she left him for someone
She'd left behind

He cried like a baby
He screamed like a panther
    In the middle of the night
And he saddled his pony
And went for a ride
It was the time of the preacher
In the year of '01
    Now the preaching is over
    And the lesson's begun

BLUE ROCK MONTANA

Well, he rode into Blue Rock
Dusty and tired
And he got him a room for the night
And he lay there in silence
With too much on his mind
Still hopin' that he was not right

But he found them that evenin'
At a tavern in town
In a quiet little out-o'-the-way place
And they smiled at each other
When he walked through the door
And they died with their smiles on their faces
They died with a smile on their face

DENVER

The bright lights of Denver
Are shining like diamonds
    Like ten thousand jewels in the sky
And it's nobody's business where you're going
Or where you come from
And you're judged by the look in your eye

She saw him that evening
In a tavern in the town
In a quiet little out-of-the-way place
And they smiled at each other
As he walked through the doors
And they danced with smiles on their faces
And they danced with a smile on their face

LAYING MY BURDENS DOWN

Well I used to walk stooped
  From the weight of my tears
  But I just started laying my burdens down
I used to duck bullets from the rifle of fear
  I just started laying my burdens down

  Oh I'm layin' 'em down
  I just started laying my burdens down
  Oh I'm layin' 'em down
  I just started laying my burdens down

The flesh ain't nothing but the bark on a tree
  I just started laying my burdens down
The tree ain't nothing but the soul in me
  ·I just started laying my burdens down

My soul took love on a helluva ride
  I just started laying my burdens down
A soul ain't nothing but the car love drives
  I just started laying my burdens down

Love said, "Mama, can I come on home?"
  I just started laying my burdens down
And God said, "Son you ain't never been gone"
  I just started laying my burdens down

THE SOUND IN YOUR MIND

Well I've been feeling a little bad
'Cause I've been feeling a little better
    Without you
It's a little like rain
But it's a lot like a sunny day
And it's hard to explain
But the sound of your name
    Don't make music anymore
And it's more than a sound
    Of a love that I lost one day

It's a little too late
To start thinking about starting all over
    I'd rather stay where I am
I can't take another slam
In the mind
I've been feeling a little bad
'Cause I've been feeling a little better
    Without you
But remember my love
    Is the sound that you hear in your mind

I've been running around
Even laughing at half of the memories
And you're not hard to remember
    I just have to think of your name
I've been feeling a little bad
'Cause I've been feeling a little better
    Without you
But remember my love
    Is the sound that you hear in your mind

And remember my love
    It's the sound that you hear in your mind

LET'S PRETEND WE'RE STRANGERS

Let's pretend we're strangers for tonight
Let's pretend we've never hurt each other
If you'll pretend I never made you cry
Then I'll pretend you didn't find another

Let's pretend our love is just beginning
Make believe that it was true love at first sight
And even though our love has never ended
Let's pretend we're strangers for tonight

RIGHT FROM WRONG

It's not right
For me to love you
It's not right to feel this way
I wish that I were far away from you
     But I know I wouldn't stay

You're not free
As someone worships you
But your love for him is gone
And when you hold me oh so close to you
Somehow I just can't distinguish right from wrong

I'll understand
If you should say good-bye
For I know that it is true
That you have more, much more to lose than I
I only have my love for you

I'm in heaven
When you're here with me
And so afraid when you are gone
And when you hold me oh so close to you
Somehow I just can't distinguish right from wrong

BLAME IT ON THE TIMES

As you sit there in your loneliness
    Confused as you might be
I'm sure a dozen questions come to mind
And if you're wondering why I left you
    After all you've done for me
I guess you'll have to blame it on the times

The many times you had your way
    No matter what the cost
And the many times you took for granted
    Love you now have lost
And if I've hurt you, darling
I don't mean to be unkind
I guess you'll have to blame it on the times

That small conceited world of yours
    Could never understand
That to want to stand alone is not a crime
And, if for one time in my life
    I'm acting like a man
I guess you'll have to blame it on the times

Blame it on the many times
    A hiding place I'd seek
Afraid to say what's on my mind
    And ashamed for being weak
So if at last I'm seeing
After so long being blind
I suppose you'll have to blame it on the times

BROKEN PROMISES

I made myself a promise
The day you put me down
That I wouldn't see you
When you came around
But here I am within your arms
The way I used to be
And I broke the promise that I made to me

They told me you were at a dance
As I prepared to go
But I made myself a promise
That I'd only say hello

I knew you'd only hurt me
But it's such sweet misery
So I broke the promise that I made to me

A broken promise always means
    Someone will surely cry
And I know who that someone's bound to be

And tomorrow I'll be sorry
That I told myself a lie
And broke the promise that I made to me

I'M BUILDING HEARTACHES

Each time that I hold you close here in my arms
    I'm building heartaches
Each time that I kiss your lips so sweet and warm
    I'm building heartaches

    And when you say you love me
    We both know it's a lie
    And just a dream from which I must awake

    And each sweet word you tell me
    Is a heartache in disguise
    So I'm building heartaches

When people ask me what I'm doing
  · Here's what I tell
    I'm building heartaches
And each kiss you give me is a tear that hasn't fell
    I'm building heartaches

I'M GONNA LOSE A LOT
OF TEARDROPS

I'm going 'round in circles
    Acting like a fool
I played the game of love
    And I don't even know the rules
I gave my heart to someone
    She broke it just today
And I'm gonna lose a lot of teardrops this way

I suppose I should be careful
    But how was I to know
She looked so sweet and innocent
    But that's the way it goes
It happens to the best of us
    At least that's what they say
But I'm gonna lose a lot of teardrops this way

Something sure had better change
    But what am I to do
Surely there's someone around
    Who needs a love that's true
But I guess I'll keep on searching
    But one thing I can say
I'm gonna lose a lot of teardrops this way

SHE'S GONE

She's gone but she was here
　　And her presence is still heavy in the air
　　What a taste of human love
Now she's gone and it don't matter anymore

Crossing dreams with our lives
　　It was more than just a woman and a man
　　It was love without the sky
Now my life will never be the same again

She is gone, she was here
　　And her presence is still heavy in the air
　　What a taste of human love
Now she's gone and it don't matter anymore

IS THE BETTER PART OVER?

Is the better part over?
Has a ragin' river turned into a stream?
Is the better part over?
Are we down to not quite saying what we mean?

And after thinkin' it over
Wouldn't you rather have the ending nice and clean?
Where love remains in all the closing scenes
If the better part's over

Why hang around
For an ending that's laden with sorrow
We both been around
And we both seen that movie before

And as much as I love you
I can't live while fearing tomorrow
If the better part's over
Then why should we try anymore?

IS THERE SOMETHING
ON YOUR MIND?

There's something on your mind
    Why don't you tell me?
You act as though your heart is miles away
I speak to you, but you don't even hear me
Don't be unkind
    Is there something on your mind?

You look at me with eyes that never see me
You're watchin' memories down in your heart
Is there someone from the past
    You can't forget, dear?
Don't be unkind
    Is there something on your mind?

Even though you've tried your best to love me
I know I can't compete with memories
So tell me now before the vows are spoken
While there's still time
    Is there something on your mind?

ANGEL FLYING TOO CLOSE
TO THE GROUND

If you would not have fallen
Then I would not have found you
Angel flying too close to the ground

And I patched up your broken wings
        And hung around a while
Trying to keep your spirits up
        And your fever down

And I knew someday that you would fly away
For love's the greatest healer to be found

So leave me if you need to
I will still remember
Angel flying too close to the ground

Fly on, fly on
        Past the speed of sound
I'd rather see you up
        Than see you down

So leave me if you need to
I will still remember
Angel flying too close to the ground

I CAN GET OFF ON YOU

Take back the weed
Take back cocaine, baby
Take back the pills,
Take back the whiskey, too
I don't need it now
'Cause your love is all I was after
I'll make it now
'Cause I can get off on you

I can get by on little or nothing at all
I can get high just thinking about you and so

Who'd ever thought
    This was something that I'd ever do
But I'm working it out and mellowing out on you

SO YOU THINK YOU'RE A COWBOY

So you think you're a cowboy
But you're only a kid
With a mind to do everything wrong
And it starts to get smoother
When the circle begins
But by the time that you get there, it's gone

So you think you're a winner
But you're losing again
The cards have already been dealt
And the hand that you're playin'
Means nothin' at all
And knowin' is all that is left

So live life as you find it
The best that you can
Tomorrow cannot right the wrong
Don't wait for tomorrow
To bring you your dreams
'Cause by the time that you get there, they're gone

TWO SIDES TO EVERY STORY

There must be two sides to every story
And who's to say who's right and who is wrong
    And I'm trying to understand
      Why you're not with me
How can we both be right
When you're still gone

It's hard to believe that it's all over
A love like ours is not supposed to die
And there must be two sides to every story
I just wish I had a chance to tell you mine

I miss you more than I could ever tell you
And we've hurt each other
      More than we could know
And there must be two sides to every story
Come on home and tell me yours
I love you so

I GUESS I'VE COME TO LIVE HERE IN YOUR EYES

I guess I've come to live here in your eyes
This must be the place called paradise
    You are so special to me
And what a special time within our lives
So I guess I've come to live here in your eyes

A thousand times I see you
And a thousand times you take my breath away
    And fears and doubts consume me
I've prayed someone will take it all away

I hope I'm here forever
But I think it's time that we both realized
But I guess I've come to live here in your eyes

IF YOU WANT ME TO LOVE YOU I WILL

I just want you to know
If you want me to love you I will
I don't want to seem forward
But to love you would be such a thrill

And the time that we spent together
So soon could be gone
And I know if we don't love together
I'll just love you alone

I know you don't know me
I know we just got here, but still
I just want you to know
If you want me to love you I will

ON THE ROAD AGAIN

On the road again
I just can't wait to get on the road again
The life I love is makin' music with my friends
And I can't wait to get on the road again

On the road again
Goin' places that I've never been
Seein' things that I may never see again
I can't wait to get on the road again

On the road again
Like a band of gypsies
We go down the highway
We're the best of friends
Insisting that the world keep turnin' our way
        And our way

Is on the road again
I just can't wait to get on the road again
The life I love is makin' music with my friends
And I can't wait to get on the road again

Album: *Tougher than Leather* *(1983)*

MY LOVE FOR THE ROSE

Was it something I did, Lord
    A lifetime ago?
Am I just now repaying a debt that I owe?

Justice, sweet justice
    You travel so slow
But you can't change my love for the rose

CHANGING SKIES

There's a bird in the sky
    Flying high, flying high
To a place from a place
    Changing skies, changing skies

There are clouds in the sky
Clouds are filled and expanding
Love like ours never dies
    Changing skies, changing skies

Little bird have you heard
Freedom lies, freedom lies
But love like ours never dies
    Just changing skies, changing skies

TOUGHER THAN LEATHER

He was tougher than leather
And he didn't care whether
    The sun shined or not
When a young kid from Cow Town
Wanted a showdown
And he was careless or just maybe forgot

But he died in a gunfight
Blinded by sunlight
    Never draw when you're facing the sun
And old tougher-than-leather
Just carved one more notch on his gun

And when he turned to go
The beautiful maiden knelt down
    Where her dead sweetheart lay
And on his breast placed a rose
While the townspeople stared in dismay

And old tougher-than-leather
Should've known better
    But he picked up the rose in his hand
And the townspeople froze
When his hands crushed the rose
And the rose petals fell in the sand

And old tougher-than-leather
Was a full-time go-getter
    The grass never grew beneath his feet
From one town to another
He would ride like the wind
But his mind kept going back to the street

Where a young cowboy died
And a young maiden cried
    And rose petals fell in the sand
And his heart had been softened
By the beautiful maid
And he knew he must see her again

Well he went back to the town
Where it all had come down
    And he searched but his search was in vain
He had wanted to find her
And say he was sorry
For causing her heart so much pain

But one night he died
From a poison inside
    Brought on by the wrong he had done
And old tougher-than-leather
Had carved his last notch on his gun

He was buried in Cowtown
Along about sundown
    Looking good in his new store-bought clothes
When the young maiden came over
And knelt down beside him
And on his lapel placed a rose

LITTLE OLD-FASHIONED KARMA

It's just a little old-fashioned karma coming down
Just a little old-fashioned justice going round
    A little bit of sowing
    And a little bit reaping
    A little bit of laughing
    And a little bit of weeping
Just a little old-fashioned karma coming down

Coming down
Coming down
Just a little old-fashioned karma
    Coming down
It really ain't hard to understand
If you're gonna dance
    You gotta pay the band

SOMEWHERE IN TEXAS (PART 1)

Somewhere in Texas
      A young cowboy dreams
Of the days when the buffalo roamed
And he wished he had lived then
      'Cause he knew he could have been
The best cowboy the world had ever known

He went dancing that night
      With his San Antone rose
The one he would marry someday
To the music of Bob Wills
      And polkas and waltzes
While beautiful time passed away

SOMEWHERE IN TEXAS (PART II)

I'm going home in this pickup
      Not knowing this stickup
Was in progress on the same side of town
By a man in a truck
      The same kind he was driving
Bad karma was soon coming down

Before the store owner died
      He had tried to describe
The man who had shot him that day
And he described to a letter
      The innocent cowboy
So he tried him and sent him away

I AM THE FOREST

I'll always be with you
For as long as you please
    For I am the forest
    But you are the trees

I'm empty without you
So come grow within me
    For I am the forest
    And you are the trees

And the heavens need romance
So love never dies
    So you be the stars, dear
    And I'll be the sky

And should any of this find us
Let them all be forewarned
    That you are the thunder
    And I am the storm

And I'll always be with you
For as long as you please
    For I am the forest
    And you are the trees

I'll always be with you
For as long as you please
    For I am the forest
    But you are the trees

NOBODY SLIDES, MY FRIEND

Nobody slides, my friend
It's a truth on which you can depend
If you're living a lie
It will eat you alive
And no lie can slide, my friend

Nobody slides, my friend
You can try it but you'll never win
You can scream, you can shout
But it all evens out
And nobody slides, my friend

Nobody slides, my friend
Listen I'll say it again
You can run, you can hide
But it's still waiting inside
And nobody slides, my friend

Album: *Songwriter (1985)*

SONGWRITER

Write it down
What you've found out
    Songwriter
Don't let it all slip away

Speak your mind
All the time
    Songwriter
Someone is listening today

So write on songwriter
Write on songwriter
Write on songwriter
Write on songwriter

WRITE YOUR OWN SONG

You're callin' us heathens
With zero respect for the law
But we're only songwriters
    Just writin' our songs, that's all
We write what we live
    And we live what we write—is that wrong?
Well, if you think it is, Mr. Music Executive
    Why don't you write your own song?

An' don't listen to mine
It might run you crazy
It might make you dwell on your feelings
    A moment too long
We're makin' you rich
An' you're already lazy
Just lay on your ass and get richer, and
    Write your own song
Mr. Purified Country
Don't you know what the whole thing's about?
Is your head up your ass
    So far that you can't pull it out?
The world's gettin' smaller
And everyone in it belongs
And if you can't see that
    Mr. Glorified Country
Why don't you write your own song?

An' don't listen to mine
It might run you crazy
It might make you dwell on your feelings
    A moment too long
We're making you rich
An' you were already lazy
Just lay on your ass and get richer, and
    Write your own song

WHY DO I HAVE TO CHOOSE?

Why do I have to choose?
And see everybody lose
Then walk around and sing the blues
Well, darling, I refuse

Love is hard to find
Love of any kind
And love like yours and mine
Creates its own design

So why do I have to choose?
And see everybody lose
Then walk around and sing the blues
Well, darling, I refuse

And when I think of her
Then I think of you
The love is not the same
But either love is true

FORGIVING YOU WAS EASY

Forgiving you was easy
But forgetting seems to take the longest time
    I just keep thinking
And your mem'ry is forever on my mind
You know I'll always love you
And I can't forget the days when you were mine
    Forgiving you is easy
    But forgetting seems to take the longest time

The bitter fruit of anger
Growing from the seeds of jealousy
    Oh what a heartache
But I forgive the things you said to me
'Cause I believe forgiving
Is the only way that I'll find peace of mind
    And forgiving you is easy
    But forgetting seems to take the longest time

The years have passed so quickly
As once again fate steals a young man's dreams
    Of all the golden years
And growing old together you and me
You asked me to forgive you
You said there was another on your mind
    Forgiving you is easy
    But forgetting seems to take the longest time

NOBODY SAID IT WAS GOING TO BE EASY

Nobody said it was going to be easy
It's only as hard as it seems
But lately it's harder than usual
Am I dreaming impossible dreams?

Will you love me forever?
    I don't even know
And I don't really care anymore
Nobody said it was going to be easy
    It never was easy before

I'M NOT TRYING TO FORGET YOU

I'm not trying to forget you anymore
I've got back into remembering
    All the love we had before
I've been trying to forget someone
That my heart still adores
So I'm not trying to forget you anymore

You're just someone who brought happiness
    Into my life
And it did not last forever
    But that's all right
We were always more than lovers
    And I'm still your friend
If I had the chance, I'd do it all again

I'm not trying to forget you anymore
I've got back into remembering
    All the love we had before
And the best day of my life
Is when you walked through my door
So I'm not trying to forget you anymore

ISLAND IN THE SEA

I am a roving cowboy
Riding all alone
And for such a roving cowboy
I've sure made myself at home

I love your sunlight
I love your flowers
I love your ocean rolling in
And for such a roving cowboy
I've sure found myself a friend

I am a cowboy
I am a sailor
I have drifted far and wide
I have crossed the seven oceans
I have crossed the Great Divide

But if you're ever looking for me
Let me tell you where I'll be
I'll be somewhere soaking up sunshine
In my island in the sea

STILL IS STILL MOVING TO ME

Still is still moving to me
And I swim like a fish in the sea
    All the time
But if that's what it takes to be free
    I don't mind

Still is still moving to me
It's hard to explain how I feel
It won't go in words, but I know that it's real
I can be moving
Or I can be still
But still is still moving to me

HEARTLAND

There's a home place under fire tonight
    In the heartland
And the bankers are takin'
    My home and my land from me
There's a big achin' hole in my chest now
    Where my heart was
And a hole in the sky where God used to be

There's a home place under fire tonight
    In the heartland
There's a well with water so bitter nobody can drink
Ain't no way to get high, and my mouth is so dry
    That I can't speak
Don't they know that I'm dyin'?
    Why's nobody cryin' for me?

My American dream
Fell apart at the seams
You tell me what it means
You tell me what it means

There's a home place under fire tonight
    In the heartland
The bankers are takin' my home and my land away
There's a young boy closin' his eyes tonight
    In the heartland
Who will wake up a man with a home and a loan he
    can't pay

His American dream
Fell apart at the seams
You tell me what it means
You tell me what it means

My American dream
Fell apart at the seams
You tell me what it means
You tell me what it means

There's a home place under fire tonight
    In the heartland

THERE IS NO EASY WAY (BUT THERE'S A WAY)

Now that we're back together
The battle is half won
We'll fight to save the part
    of yesterday

I know it won't be easy
But at least we have begun
There is no easy way
    but there is a way

We both could use some understanding—
    trust within
And the journey
Of a thousand miles begins
    With just one step

And is love not worth the price
    we'll have to pay
These is no easy way
    but there is a way

HEEBIE JEEBIE BLUES

Well I'm standing on Broadway looking down Main
Looking at that girl I'll never see again

    I'm checking out
    I'm checking out
    I gotta get on the move
    I've got the Heebie Jeebie Blues

Well now I hate to go
    You're a good ole girl, I know
You got the right string but the wrong yo-yo

Sometimes I'm wishy washy
    I just can't hang around
I've got another baby waiting in another town

I may be back someday, right now I just can't say
Something keeps on pulling me down the other way

I gotta get on the move
I've got the Heebie Jeebie Blues

VALENTINE

Valentine
Won't you be my valentine
And introduce your heart to mine
    And be my valentine

Summertime
We could run and play like summertime
With storybooks and nursery rhymes
    So be my valentine

Candy heart
If anyone could, you could have a candy heart
You're the sweetest of all sweethearts
Won't you give your heart to me?

Can't you see
I love you valentine
Won't you be my valentine
And won't you share your space with mine
    Be my valentine

Candy heart
If anyone could, you could have a candy heart
You're the sweetest of all sweethearts
Won't you give your heart to me
Can't you see
I love you, valentine

Won't you be my valentine
And introduce your heart to mine
    Be my valentine

THERE'S WORSE THINGS THAN BEING ALONE

We finally said all our final goodbyes
And tear after tear fell from everyone's eyes
      It was just like a funeral
      Where nobody dies
There's worse things than being alone

There's worse things than being alone
Like a full house and nobody home
      If the feeling keeps changing
      Then something's gone wrong
There's worse things than being alone

I'm well past my half way in time
But I still have a lot on my mind
      But there's one thing for certain
      And it's beyond right or wrong
There's worse things than being alone

Afterword

In the spring of 1973 I moved to Nashville and landed in an apartment with Geoff, an Englishman who was a Waylon Jennings fanatic. Kinky Friedman had just moved out of the apartment but there were "Texas Jewboys" stickers all over the walls and one in the commode. Billy Swan lived upstairs, while the "E-Z Method Driving School" had its headquarters just below.

The buzz in Nashville that spring was about a big concert planned in Texas for the Fourth of July and organized by Willie Nelson. At this point the old timers and the Grand Ole Opry had fallen out of fashion with the new breed taking over Nashville; it was Kris Kristofferson who was the hero, not Roy Acuff. Willie Nelson had a cult status; he had always been the insider's favorite, the songwriter's songwriter, and had just released two stunning albums, *Shotgun Willie* and *Phases and Stages*. So I hitchhiked down to Dripping Springs to watch the show.

By noon I'd managed to get to Dripping Springs from Austin. The sun was hot, the land was rocky and rolling and the people were heading into the concert like streams of water flowing to a pool. The music had started before I got there and it was after midnight when it finished. Along the way I saw those who became known as leaders in the "outlaw" movement perform. The emcee was Willie Nelson, a genial, relaxed, easy-going fellow who introduced acts and played a helluva show of his own. That was my introduction to Willie Nelson.

Later I went to other Fourth of July picnics—as an insider with a backstage pass—but I'll always remember that first one best. I also wrote some stories on

Willie, interviewed him a time or two, and wrote the liner notes on two albums RCA released in the mid-1970s after he'd left the label. Texas, especially the Austin area, was a magic place in the mid-1970s and Willie Nelson performances there during that time were more than performances, they were *events*. I saw Willie play at the Texas Opry House, at outdoor events, and in small clubs. It was always magic. And I also saw him perform in Nashville before a huge crowd at the Municipal Auditorium. Willie had returned a conquering hero; when he walked to the microphone with his guitar his first words were "Well, hello there. My, it's been a long, long time." The crowd went berserk, screaming and cheering.

This is more than a book; it is an honor and a privilege. Willie Nelson is one of the finest songwriters of this century and I've collected these lyrics to show the best of his songs. Lord knows these aren't all the songs Willie has written—he guesses he's written "thousands" and there's fewer than two hundred here. But it's a complete book in that it includes the songs he's written that he has recorded and released commercially—and then some. I reasoned that if Willie thought enough of them to put them on his own albums, then he must've thought they were something special. I did, however, include some very early songs that surfaced on some forgotten tapes which were released on small labels in order to show examples of some of his earliest commerical songs.

First, I would like to thank my editor at St. Martin's, Cal Morgan, for believing in this project and for always pushing and prodding me to make it better. I also appreciate the support of Jim Fitzgerald, also at St. Martin's, and my hard working agent, Madeleine Morel, for pulling it all together.

I must thank the Country Music Foundation for their excellent archives, and especially Ronnie Pugh and Bob Pinson for their help as well as some enjoyable lunches. This book simply would not have been possible without that marvelous institution. Obviously, I owe a great debt to Willie Nelson, who read the manuscript and talked with me about his songwriting. Also Mark Rothbaum, Willie's manager; Donna Hilley, head of Sony/Tree Publishing Company, which owns Willie's early copyrights (and who has been incredibly encouraging and supportive throughout this project); Evelyn Shriver, who handles publicity for Willie and always managed to get us connected when it was necessary; Marsha Costa with Warner/Chappell; and Lisa Grandee with Windswept Publishing, who handles Willie's later songs. The publicity department at CBS/Sony supplied me with some Willie Nelson CDs along the way, which made life easier, and Roy Wunsch was always available for additional material if needed.

The folks at Belmont University where I work are extremely helpful and supportive, especially Bob Mulloy and Cliff Eubanks. And doing a book like this would simply be impossible without the help of Pat Hamilton, Christi Weston and Amy Michelle Grimes, who have dropped what they were doing and taken care of my emergencies on many occasions.

On a personal level I must thank my wife Jackie, who is always encouraging and understanding while I'm struggling with a book, and my children, Delaney, Jesse, Eli and Alex, for taking my mind off work.

1988); "Night Life" (Willie Nelson, Walt Breeland, and Paul
Buskirk) (renewed 1992); "Misery Mansion" (Willie Nelson and
Hank Craig) (renewed 1989).

"And So Will You My Love" (1965;
renewed); "Any Old Arms Won't Do" (Willie Nelson and Hank
Cochran) (1964; renewed); "Are You Ever Coming Home?"
(Willie Nelson and Hank Cochran) (1964; renewed); "Are You
Sure?" (Willie Nelson and Buddy Emmons) (1962; renewed);
"Blame It on the Times" (1978); "Both Ends of the Candle"
(1964; renewed); "Broken Promises" (Willie Nelson and Hank
Cochran) (1978; renewed); "Buddy" (1965; renewed);
"Congratulations" (1961; renewed); "Country Willie" (1961;
renewed); "Crazy" (1961; renewed); "Darkness on the Face of
the Earth" (1961; renewed); "December Day" (1968); "Did I
Ever Love You?" (1966; renewed); "The End of Understanding"
(1962; renewed); "Everything But You" (1962; renewed); "Face
of a Fighter" (1962; renewed); "Funny How Time Slips Away"
(1961; renewed); "The Ghost" (1962; renewed); "Go Away"
(1961; renewed); "Good Times" (1968); "Half a Man" (1962;
renewed); "Happiness Lives Next Door" (1962; renewed);
"Healing Hands of Time" (1964; renewed); "Heartaches of a
Fool" (Willie Nelson, Walt Breeland and Paul Buskirk) (1961;
renewed); "Hello Walls" (1961; renewed); "Hold Me Tighter"
(1962; renewed); "Home Is Where You're Happy" (1966;
renewed); "Home Motel" (1962; renewed); "How Long Is
Forever?" (1961; renewed); "I Can't Find the Time" (Willie
Nelson and Hank Cochran) (1961; renewed); "I Didn't Sleep a
Wink" (Willie Nelson and Jimmy Day) (1961; renewed); "I
Don't Feel Anything" (1967); "I Gotta Get Drunk" (1963;
renewed); "I Just Can't Let You Say Goodbye" (1965; renewed);
"I Don't Understand" (1964; renewed); "I Just Stopped By"
(1962; renewed); "I Let My Mind Wander" (1966; renewed); "I
Never Cared for You" (1964; renewed); "I'll Stay Around"
(Willie Nelson and Hank Cochran) (1962; renewed); "I'm
Building Heartaches" (Willie Nelson and Hank Cochran) (1978);
"I'm Gonna Lose a Lot of Teardrops" (1978); "In God's Eyes"
(1961; renewed); "Is There Something on Your Mind?" (1978);
"It Should Be Easier Now" (1963; renewed); "It's Not for Me to
Understand" (1963; renewed); "Jimmy's Road" (1968); "Kneel at
the Feet of Jesus" (1962; renewed); "Laying My Burdens
Down" (1976); "Let's Pretend We're Strangers" (1977); "Little
Things" (Willie Nelson and Shirley Nelson) (1968); "The Local
Memory" (1963; renewed); "Lonely Little Mansion" (1961;
renewed); "Mean Old Greyhound Bus" (Willie Nelson and
Hank Cochran); "The Message" (1966; renewed); "A Moment
Isn't Very Long" (1961; renewed); "Mr. Record Man" (1961;
renewed); "My Own Peculiar Way" (1964; renewed); "New Way
to Cry" (1961; renewed); "Night Life" (Willie Nelson, Walt
Breeland and Paul Buskirk) (1962); "No Tomorrow in Sight"

(1961; renewed); "Once Alone" (1962; renewed); "One Day at a Time" (1964; renewed); "One in a Row" (1966; renewed); "One Step Beyond" (1961; renewed); "Opportunity to Cry" (1963; renewed); "Pages" (Willie Nelson, Shirley Nelson and Lana Nelson) (1968; renewed); "The Part Where I Cry" (1961; renewed); "Permanently Lonely" (1963; renewed); "Pretty Paper" (1962; renewed); "Pride Wins Again" (1962; renewed); "Ridgetop" (1964; renewed); "Right from Wrong" (1977); "Sad Songs and Waltzes" (1964; renewed); "She's Not for You" (1962; renewed); "She's Still Gone" (Willie Nelson and Shirley Nelson) (1968); "Slow Down Old World" (1967; renewed); "So Much to Do" (1965; renewed); "So You Think You're a Cowboy" (Willie Nelson and Hank Cochran) (1979); "Some Other Time" (1961; renewed); "Something to Think About" (1966; renewed); "Suffer in Silence" (1962; renewed); "Take My Word" (1962; renewed); "Thanks Again" (1962; renewed); "There Goes a Man" (1962; renewed); "Things to Remember" (1961; renewed); "Three Days" (1962; renewed); "To Make a Long Story Short (She's Gone)" (Willie Nelson and Fred Foster) (1964; renewed); "Today's Gonna Make a Wonderful Yesterday" (1966; renewed); "Touch Me" (1961; renewed); "Undo the Right" (1961; renewed); "Waiting Time" (1961; renewed); "Wake Me When It's Over" (1962; renewed); "What Can You Do to Me Now?" (Willie Nelson and Hank Cochran) (1970); "Where My House Lives" (1961; renewed); "Who Do I Know in Dallas?" (1968; renewed); "Within Your Crowd" (1962; renewed); "You Left a Long, Long Time Ago" (1964; renewed); "You Ought to Hear Me Cry" (1967); "You Took My Happy Away" (1963; renewed); "You Wouldn't Cross the Street (to Say Goodbye)" (1962; renewed); "You'll Always Have Someone" (1964; renewed).

Circles, Cycles and Scenes" (1972); "Pick Up the Tempo" (1974); "Pretend I Never Happened" (1972); "Remember the Good Times" (1971); "She's Gone" (1978); "Shotgun Willie" (1973); "Sister's Coming Home" (1972); "Somewhere in Texas" (1982); "Songwriter" (1984); "The Sound in Your Mind" (1976); "Stay Away from Lonely Places" (1972); "Still Is Still Moving to Me" (1989); "Summer of Roses" (1971); "There Is No Easy Way (But There's a Way)" (1982); "These Are Difficult Times" (1976); "Time of the Preacher" (1975); "Tougher than Leather" (1982); "Two Sides to Every Story" (1980); "Walkin' " (1974); "Where do You Stand?" (1974); "Where's the Show?" (1971); "Why Do I Have to Choose?" (1983); "Will You Remember Mine?" (1973); "The Words Don't Fit the Picture" (1972); "Write Your Own Song" (1982); "Yesterday's Wine" (1971).